His
Guiding
Hand

His Guiding Hand

The Story of a Life Blessed

ORVILLE MERILLAT

Foreword by
D. James Kennedy, Ph.D.

P.O. Box 40, Fort Lauderdale, FL 33302

Published by Coral Ridge Ministries
P.O. Box 40, Fort Lauderdale, Florida 33302

Christian Family Foundation
1800 West U.S. 223
Adrian, MI 49221

Unless otherwise indicated, all Scripture is from the Holy Bible: New
International Version, copyright © 1973, 1978 by International Bible
Society. Used by permission of Zondervan Bible Publishers.

Printed in the United States of America

Many thanks to our family and friends who have contributed to our lives, our testimony, and ultimately to this book. We dedicate it to you—for the glory of the Lord Jesus Christ

Contents

A Higher Purpose

Senator Dan Coats

THE FULFILLMENT of the American Dream is often measured in material terms—the extent of one's material prosperity and the degree to which he or she has risen from humble financial circumstances.

These measurements are, at best, incomplete. While those who have succeeded in building successful enterprises deserve credit for their dedication and hard work, to imply that the American dream is merely about the accumulation of wealth reflects a shallow understanding of what that dream truly means.

Orville and Ruth Merillat embody the best of the American dream. Yes, they have been successful entrepreneurs—so successful that the original Merillat woodworking shop in Adrian, Michigan, has expanded to eleven plants in seven states and become the world's largest cabinet-making company.

Moreover, Orville and Ruth have provided employment for thousands and their company offers top-quality merchandise for homes and businesses across the country and around the world. For these remarkable contributions to our society alone they merit high praise.

But the Merillats learned early the truth of the words of Jesus—"a man's life does not consist in the abundance of his possessions." Their lives are not studies of the pursuit of wealth for its own sake, but of how people of faith can pursue professional excellence for a higher purpose than an ever-larger business.

Orville receives the Michigan Small Business Person
of the Year award in 1977.

The Merillats have served their community, their state, their country and their world with a selfless generosity. From founding a 700-student Christian school and building the Christian Family Centre to promote Christian family values to funding an obstetrics ward in Narsapur, India, Orville and Ruth have lived as testimonies to the value of faithful stewardship.

Yes, the professional awards have been many—President of the National Kitchen Cabinet Association, Michigan Small Business Person of the Year, and designation as Laypersons of the Year by the National Association of Evangelicals, to name a few. But Orville and Ruth, in their over half-century of marriage, have been outstanding examples of the worth of knowing God—and it is this legacy that is more enduring than any external achievement, however noteworthy, ever could be.

His Guiding Hand is an apt title for this book, which I know will encourage all its readers to trust that hand more completely. I applaud Orville and Ruth for lives that bear the imprint of consistent obedience, and rejoice with them in reflecting on the goodness of a gracious Lord.

An American Success Story

D. James Kennedy, Ph.D.

ON A beautiful summer evening in 1988, an Orlando, Florida, ballroom was filled to capacity for the closing banquet and awards ceremony of the 46th Annual Convention of the National Association of Evangelicals. As the spotlight moved back and forth across the room, it shone on many of the most notable Christian leaders in America. In fact, guests had come from coast to coast and from around the world to participate in these events. Tonight they would recognize the individuals selected as Laypersons of the Year.

As the presentation approached, the audience

scanned the program which listed previous honorees. In 1982 the award had gone to Dr. James Dobson of Focus on the Family; in 1983 to Chuck Colson, who heads Prison Fellowship ministries. In 1984 Sen. William Armstrong was honored, and in 1985 Joni Eareckson Tada, whose powerful books and syndicated radio broadcasts have given her a unique ministry to the disabled, received the award. Businessman Stanley Tam was honored in 1986 and Representative Dan Coats in 1987. All in all, it was an impressive list.

When the big moment arrived, President Ray Hughes came forward to read the citation, and he called out the names of Orville and Ruth Merillat of Adrian, Michigan, Co-Laypersons of the Year for 1988. For most people in the hall that night, this was the first time they had ever heard the names of the honorees. But as the tribute was read, acknowledging the achievements of this husband and wife team, there was a respectful silence.

"The term 'quality' is defined in part as 'superiority in kind' and 'a degree of excellence.' It might be more properly defined, however, as a synonym for Merillat . . ." Reading from the citation, the speaker described a couple who had grown a family business into a manufacturing giant, the leader in their industry. He described a couple who went on to establish the Christian Family Foundation and the Merillat Foundation located in Adrian, Michigan. They pioneered and developed the Christian Family Centre in their home town and a large, modern Christian school complex, which today serves approximately 700 students in grades pre-kindergarten through twelve.

Beyond these activities, the Merillats were also involved in countless ministries through their private and confidential benevolences. Even the partial list mentioned that night was impressive. And while this was the first time many people were made aware of the achievements of this dynamic couple, it surely would not be the last.

Jim and Anne Kennedy with Orville and Ruth Merillat in the Christian Family Centre (Scott Hall Photography).

Since that time, I have come to know the Merillats much better, and I have developed a deep respect and admiration for the work they are doing in support of the Christian family. I am proud to call Orville and Ruth my friends, and I am especially pleased for Coral Ridge Ministries to be able to participate in telling their life story to a much larger audience.

Many people who were not at the ceremony that night in Orlando first heard of the work being done by the Merillats through the spotlight article on the Christian Family Centre in the February 1991 issue of the Focus on the Family magazine. This was the first time their story had actually been told in print.

The sight of the sprawling regional complex built by the Merillats in rural Adrian, Michigan, is, indeed, striking. The more than 4,000 members of this facility have access to a gymnasium, swimming pool, bowling alley, racquetball courts, a complete fitness center, full-service dining and banquet facilities, and a 700-seat auditorium which hosts a wide range of top-notch performers and family events—all in a wholesome, Christian environment.

The magazine's description of the center as a state-of-the-art entertainment and education complex for Christian families in southeastern Michigan provoked a flood of response from all over the country. But that article also drew attention to the testimony of two people who, quietly and lovingly, have invested their lives in the kingdom of God.

A Story of Commitment

The life story of Orville Merillat is a genuine adventure. It is not just the story of a boy who ran away from home to find excitement in the Wild West, or of a young sailor who came ashore with Gen. Douglas MacArthur in The Philippines. It is not simply the story of a talented carpenter who saw his dream grow into the largest, most successful company in his industry. But it is, above all, the story of a man and woman who decided to take God at His word, to invest their hopes and their resources in Him, and to trust Him for the results.

Today, the small business Orville and Ruth Merillat founded in 1946 has become Merillat Industries, the largest manufacturer of kitchen and bath cabinetry in the United States. Their unique designs, patented components, and vertical integration make Merillat the undisputed king of cabinets. In 1973 they were fifteenth in this industry, and by 1990 were more than 50 percent beyond their nearest competitor in sales. Merillat is the clear leader in a $4 billion industry.

The company now operates eleven plants in seven states, with more than 2.5 million square feet of manufacturing and assembly space under roof. Purchased by giant Masco Corporation in 1985, the firm is still headed by Richard Merillat, son of the founders, who grew up with the business.

Looking at the growth of Merillat over the past forty-six years, it would be easy to see how hard work and persistence have paid off. It would be easy to show how the American dream has smiled on yet another Midwest farm boy, and how shrewd management and smart timing led to the birth of an empire. But that is not the Merillat story.

The Merillat story is the story of a series of personal

commitments and the impact they have had over many years. It is the story of the sense of responsibility which made Orville Merillat, first, a good carpenter, and then a caring employer. It is the story of a production incentive program, called the Trust and Share Program, through which the Merillats have shared profits from increased productivity with employees for more than twenty-five years. And it is the story of faithful stewardship and Christian giving based on the literal application of Scripture.

The impact of the Merillats' story is being felt today in many places around the globe. It can be felt in the new obstetrics ward funded by the Merillats at the Narsapur Hospital in India, and in farm development projects in Sierra Leone, West Africa, where missionaries supported by the Merillat Foundation are now able to travel to remote tribal villages to clean up water systems and introduce self-help projects to improve living conditions for the people of Africa. It can be felt in helping Life Ministries in Tokyo, Japan, serve pastors, missionaries, and young people from a half dozen Asian nations.

Their impact can be seen in the new sports center built by the Merillats at Adrian College. Other facilities they have funded at Asbury College in Wilmore, Kentucky, Huntington College in Huntington, Indiana, and Siena Heights College in Adrian also help tell the Merillat story. It can also be seen at the Michindoh Camp and Conference Center, a beautiful 243-acre year-round Christian retreat serving Michigan, Indiana, and Ohio and supported by the Merillat Foundation.

Not least, their impact is continually visible today in

those eleven plants in Michigan, South Dakota, Ohio, Massachusetts, Virginia, Minnesota, and Nevada where workers are respected as equals and paid as partners. The success of the Merillats' Trust and Share Program offers a dynamic formula for labor and management cooperation which could revolutionize American business. Orville Merillat believes that God has told him to describe this program in detail so that other companies can profit from his example; so that America may yet be revitalized and renewed.

The Trust and Share Program

A first time visitor at a Merillat plant is immediately struck by the high level of enthusiasm and employee morale. I am told that absenteeism is virtually non-existent in the Merillat organization, and there is a genuine sense of teamwork among the workers. The President's Club honors employees who have missed less than an hour of work over the past year, and in some plants more than half of the employees are members. Underlying this upbeat atmosphere is the knowledge that employees are paid competitively and that increased production means higher wages for everyone. Orville Merillat says, "It's a simple formula: trusting and sharing."

Reed Larson, president of the National Right to Work Committee in Washington, D.C., commented recently on the Merillat Trust and Share Program. "I have never encountered such an extremely high level of cooperation between labor and management," he said. "Where the plan is implemented with a spirit of fairness and mutual cooperation, as it is in

Merillat Industries, it will become a dynamic force in creating a cooperative and productive work environment."

In an address to industry leaders, Lawrence W. Reed, President of the Mackinac Center for Public Policy, observed that it is this high level of labor/management cooperation at Merillat Industries which "gives this dynamic company its cutting edge."

The inspiration for this amazing program came in 1967, when Orville Merillat realized that low morale, lost man-hours, excessive breaks, and work stoppages were costing them money. On average, the company was losing thirty minutes of production time every day, and ultimately the customer was paying for lost productivity in the higher cost of goods. This dilemma set Merillat to thinking.

Based on past output, he determined the base production levels for the company and quickly recognized that lost time could be calculated in terms of manufactured goods. By the same token, he realized that while low productivity meant fewer goods and lost revenues, increased efficiency could mean more goods and higher revenues. And either way, the basic cost of labor remained the same.

"The material and overhead are a constant part of each dollar of product," he reasoned, "however, eight hours of labor remains the same regardless of output." What he needed was some sort of incentive to encourage the workers to be more efficient. "It came to me that sharing the labor and fringe portion of each dollar of increased production would be an equitable method of helping everybody."

After careful consideration, Orville called his employees together and offered them a new proposition. "If production stays about where it is or even drops slightly," he said, "nothing will change; but if production increases and quality remains high, the company and the employees will split the savings from the increase. That means, if we produce 105 units in an eight-hour day instead of the basic 100, we'll split the savings from the additional five units 50/50." It was a novel idea, but someone finally spoke up, "What have we got to lose?" They decided to give Orville's idea a try.

"I thought a dollar in the hand would be more convincing than my words," he said, "so I told them how much bonus they were earning every day and paid them their bonus every week. After just three or four weeks of steadily growing paychecks, I could see an immediate difference in productivity and attitudes."

What Orville saw was not just harder work but better work, more interest, and greater efficiency. "Not only did they put the lost thirty minutes back to work, but the ingenuity of the employees increased dramatically." Coffee breaks became coffee breaks once again, and cigarette breaks and restroom breaks dropped to a minimum.

Unexpected Dividends

As the plan began to produce visible results, other factors came into play. First, increased production called for newer and better equipment, so the company began to upgrade its machinery and systems. Again, productivity increased. Second, peer pressure became a much greater factor on the plant floor; consequently, managers were soon able to spend more time making sure that their supply channels and production systems were working properly. Keeping adequate supplies on hand was a growing concern.

Third, to show that the "Trust and Share" relationship was genuine, all workers were put on salary. There would be no hourly workers as long as the employees wanted it that way. Today, ten of Merillat's eleven plants continue on that basis: only the Adrian plant has chosen to retain the hourly system.

To make sure that increased production did not mean lower quality, labor and management agreed that the expense of any product which had to be scrapped would come out of the bonus plan; and the expense of any product which actually made it to the customer's dock and was then rejected because of quality problems would be deducted from the plan at double its production cost. This offered a good practical incentive and, as a result, every worker became a quality inspector.

The bottom line for most employees is a valuable, visible reward for a job well done, paid on a weekly basis. Wayne Blamer, an employee at Merillat's Jackson, Ohio, plant, told economist Lawrence Reed, "Our incentive pay just about buys the groceries every week."

Since 1967 the plan has generated millions in bonus pay. In 1990 alone, Merillat paid more than $7 million in production bonuses to its 2,500 employees. "In addition," says President Richard Merillat, "we're gaining their trust, their ingenuity, and their spirit to produce more than they would with an hourly wage."

The Trust and Share Plan, along with vertical integration and a favorable economic climate, produced tremendous growth in this small company. Due to the cooperation of the partners on the floor and the efficiency of new equipment, output per man-hour rose dramatically.

Even with multiple plants and inter-dependent manufacturing systems, corporate executives insist that the company's high level of productivity could only be accomplished through the cooperation and open communication which is a hallmark of the Trust and Share Program.

Richard Krull, manager of the company's particleboard plant in Rapid City agrees that clear communication is the key to employee cooperation. "We knew," he said, "that if we communicated effectively, we would build strong bridges that would allow for a healthy interchange of ideas and encourage a shared feeling of commitment and teamwork. And share they did. They shared their thoughts, their skills, their talents, and their pride. They showed us determination and a sincere desire to contribute to the success of their company."

He adds, "Today there is little that we do not share with our employees, and there is little that they won't share with us."

A Spirit of Cooperation

John D. Lewis remembers his first meeting with Orville Merillat in 1976, just nine years after the inception of the Trust and Share Program. "I found Orville to be an uncomplicated direct man with an attention to detail," he said. "The thing I remember about that meeting was his philosophy. To me it meant trusting the involvement and responsibility of making the company successful to all of his employees and then sharing the benefits in the form of an incentive program once we had accomplished this. I remember thinking that this attitude toward employees was too good to be true."

But Lewis found out just how true it was. He has spent fifteen productive years with Merillat, and today he is manager of the company's Jackson, Ohio, plant. "This story is not singular in occurring," he says. "My staff, as with most of the others, could recite it over and over again. . . . To sum it all up, Trust and Share really has worked for us."

Orville Merillat has said that the "partnership" relationship is the real secret of Trust and Share. In an address before government and business leaders, which included Michigan Governor John Engler, Orville said, "Thanks to the Trust and Share Program, we experienced a 25 percent increase in production in all those plants. In order to get that kind of increase it takes the ingenuity of the worker, the supervisors, the engineers, the customers, and everyone else in the product cycle. The end result of the increased productivity is in the product itself, and everyone in the cycle shares not only in the work but in the rewards."

Another plant manager, Pete Palpant, remembers the day he came to work at Merillat more than twenty years ago. He started out drilling holes in cabinet frames. It was boring work, he recalls, but his supervisor explained the bonus and incentive features of the Trust and Share Program and when he saw the actual cash bonus on his first paycheck, he became a believer. "In the weeks to follow," he said, "I found that the Merillats were true to their word, that the better the company did, the better I would do. That day the company passed the test!"

But Palpant must have passed the test as well, for over the years he learned the system, developed more and more supervisory skills, and today he is plant manager. "This farm boy without a college education," he said, "is trusted to operate and make decisions in a multi-million dollar factory. Cabinet assembly time has gone from about five minutes to less than one minute per cabinet, and the quality of Merillat cabinetry is the envy of our competitors."

Palpant has also seen the specific benefits to the employees increase over the years. The Trust and Share Plan has been well received, absenteeism is around 1 percent, and employee turnover is nil. We find ourselves in a very unique position compared to companies around us. Our problems revolve around how to keep things out of the way of the employees so they can progress.

"The incentive and recognition programs work!" he added. "There is trust and mutual respect. In more ways than one, you get out of this organization what you put into it."

As remarkable as such testimonies may seem, they are the rule in all eleven plants. Consider the comments of Ray Welsh: "I am an employee of Merillat Industries at the Adrian plant and have worked there for thirty-six years. I started out as an assembler and worked my way through various positions and now I am the plant manager." Like John Lewis and Pete Palpant, Welsh has seen the effectiveness of the Trust and Share program from the ground up. "From an employee viewpoint, the incentive system allowed me to see each week that I was contributing to the success of the company and at the same time sharing in the profit. It gave me a sense of working for myself. I think, to some extent, it helped me to be more businesslike and to look at my job in a more serious manner. . . . I had a feeling of ownership."

The Windows of Heaven

Even a brief glimpse at the life of Orville and Ruth Merillat, at their practical faith and generosity in business, helps explain their conspicuous success. From the first, Orville believed in trusting his employees to do the best possible job; and he believed in giving them the opportunity to share in the rewards. As an accountant and bookkeeper for the Merillat enterprises over the years, Ruth helped manage that process and ensured that the resources of their various interests and endeavors were used wisely.

Orville's life story, in the following chapters, is the story of a life built on trust. First, it is the story of how he came to trust in his family and in himself; second it is the story of how he came to trust in God; and finally, it is the story of how he expressed that trust through his Christian faith, his business principles, and through unselfish philanthropy.

Lois Lawrence Chester, the writer who worked closely with Orville in relating and writing this story, is an employee of the Christian Family Centre in Adrian, Michigan. After months of transcribing and composing, Lois came to understand the essential character of Orville Merillat with new insight. She calls it "faithfulness," and she says that such faithfulness is infectious.

"Faithfulness begets faithfulness," Lois says. "When someone is committed to faithful service to Jesus Christ and practices it daily, other faithful servants are drawn together with them to do a great work for God's glory."

The source of the Merillats' faithfulness can be better understood, she explains, when you realize that their life verse is Malachi 3:10, which says:

> "Bring all the tithes into the storehouse, that there may be food in My house, and test Me now in this," says the Lord of hosts, "and see if I will not open for you the windows of heaven and pour out for you such blessing that there will not be room enough to receive it" (NKJV).

"When I was first honored by being introduced to Orville and Ruth Merillat," Lois Chester said, "never did I dream that their vision would spread like a wildfire through so many people, including me. Their love for Christ, their willingness to share with others, their passion for excellence, their eagerness to do as much as good stewards can do for the cause of Christ while there is yet time, is the example and testimony of their lives and lips."

Since coming to know the Merillats, Lois has seen thousands, even tens of thousands, of lives touched by their vision. She can see the children in the adjoining Lenawee Christian School, where her own children attend, being blessed on a daily basis. And when her daughter leaves for her first semester at Huntington College in the fall, Lois will experience yet another blessing from the Merillats.

"I was a homemaker and volunteer with only a high school education and no formally developed skills when I first met Orville and Ruth," Lois said. "But the Merillats showed me that God can use ordinary people, just as He has used them, and just as He is using me today. We're nothing special in and of ourselves, but God is looking for willing hands, hearts, and talents, to make us partners of His will.

"That's what Orville wants us all to be," she says, "and that is what his story is about. A simple man willing to use his talents for the Lord, to the betterment of mankind. It is my prayer that his story will inspire others to commit their lives and talents to Christ: being faithful, letting nothing deter you from the partnership of the cause of Christ."

Like Lois Chester, James McClellan, Jr., Executive Director of the Christian Family Foundation, works closely with Orville and Ruth Merillat on a day-to-day basis. McClellan believes that the Merillats' faithfulness is the result of their simple obedience to Scripture.

"Obeying God's Word!" he said. "That's the thought that comes to mind when I think about the faithful stewards who are the subject of this book. What a privilege for me to be so closely associated with this special couple and to see them operate from God's perspective, using what He has blessed them with to make a difference in the lives of others."

Taking God at His Word

It is surely true that we can judge a Christian's faithfulness by what he does with the resources God gives him. But no matter how generous the Merillats have been, God's blessing in their lives always seemed to be greater. How do the Merillats explain it? "God's shovel was simply bigger than mine," says Orville. But the convincing evidence of the truth of Malachi 3:10 has taught him an important lesson: "Just love the Lord, and trust Him to meet your needs. Give from what you have, little or much."

When my associates and I spoke with Orville recently, we asked him how he would respond to so many people today who find themselves deep in debt, their dreams still unfulfilled, who have concluded that it would be impossible for them to give freely to God. Tithing is out of the question.

Orville's answer was thoughtful but direct: "Every journey starts with a first step. No one else can solve your problem for you; you've got to solve it for yourself. But what does the Bible say? Does it say wait until you're out of debt before giving to the Lord? No, it says bring your tithes into the storehouse. But it also says that if you fail to do that you are robbing God.

"If you're in debt $10,000 and you're only making $10,000 or $12,000 a year, I would say this, trust Him! That's what He says: 'test Me now in this,' says the Lord of hosts, 'and see if I will not open for you the windows of heaven and pour out for you such blessing that there will not be room enough to receive it.'"

Surely the story of the widow's mite in the Bible confirms Orville's view. As Jesus sat in the temple He observed a rich man making a lavish show of his wealth, placing a large sum of money in the offering box. After him came a poor widow who gave a tiny, almost worthless coin. But Jesus saw the heart of the matter. What the rich man gave was a tiny, insignificant fraction of his vast wealth; what the widow gave was all she possessed on earth. The rich man's gift was

Dr. Kennedy displays a model Merillat kitchen.

for show; the widow's gift was for the love of God in her heart. Jesus saw both gifts, and what he valued most was the widow's simple gift of love.

During our discussion, Orville commented on this truth. "When God tells us to bring our gifts into the storehouse, He is not just referring to dollars. In our society today, we tend to think too much of the dollar. You've heard it called the Almighty Dollar. Most people refer to the value of things in terms of dollars and cents, but that's not the only measure. This Christian Family Centre, for example, is never going to make a penny, but it's a good investment. What the Bible says is that if we trust God and honor Him with our tithe, He will pour out a blessing upon us. How much simpler can He make it?"

Orville went on to say, "When Ruth and I give money to support some work or some project, it's nice to know that the money will help. We get letters from people telling us how our gifts have helped them, but it's not the money that really counts." After a brief, emotional pause, he placed his hand over his heart and added, "It's the feeling here that counts."

Later, James McClellan, Jr. told me that he has learned so much about the love of God just by watching Orville and Ruth and observing how they think. "I am continually amazed," he said, "by the humility exhibited by this dear brother and sister in the Lord. They are held in such high esteem in so many places for all they have done; yet their response to any praise directed at them is simply to say that they are just trying to be faithful to God. They will accept no personal praise."

Today, McClellan reports, the generosity of the Merillats has set into motion a cycle of blessings through the Christian Family Foundation. "The mission of this foundation," he says, "is to establish an environment where strong family relationships can be built and fostered. The Merillats have challenged us to follow the same principles that helped make their cabinet business the best in the business. Their motto has always been, 'Do your best, and then some.' We try to follow that advice, and I have discovered that it's the 'then some' that makes the difference."

The Challenge of True Faith

If you grew up anywhere near a Christian church, you have probably heard the words of the old hymn, "He leads His dear children along." When I pause, as I have often done lately, to consider the hand of God in the lives of Orville and Ruth Merillat, I think of these words. God is merciful and gentle to those who trust Him, to those who come to Him in true faithfulness.

With the promise of Malachi 3:10, that God will pour out a blessing upon those who bring the tithes into the storehouse, these loving people have put God to the test, even as He challenged them to do, and they have found Him as good as His Word.

Among the many others who have taken this risk of faith are men such as J. C. Penney, who built a department store empire; Robert G. LeTourneau, whose incredible story is told in the book, Mover of Men and Mountains; and Stanley Tam, who often said, as the title of his book proclaims, "God Owns My Business." Each was a captain of industry who was blessed richly according to their faith. Orville and Ruth Merillat surely fall within this category.

As you turn now to Orville's life story, it is his sincere hope, and mine, that you will find here an inspiring example of God's faithfulness and a challenge to apply the lessons within the following pages to your own life.

Above all, I hope you will see that what often seems accidental and coincidental in our lives is, in fact, the very hand of God. When people deny the power of God in their lives and attempt to live as a law unto themselves, they hinder and invalidate the good things God wants to do for and through them. But if they are obedient, faithful, and simple in their trust, even as Orville and Ruth have been throughout their lives, they too will find God as good as His Word . . . and then some.

Miracles Still Happen

W HEN I opened my little woodworking shop in 1946, I had no idea what challenges lay ahead of me. Today, nearly a half century later, the company has become an enormous success. Our tiny cabinet shop is now Merillat Industries, America's number one manufacturer of kitchen and bath cabinetry for the home, with eleven plants nationwide. The Merillat name and its quality products are known to homebuilders in all fifty states, as well as in South Korea and Canada. Merillat cabinets are advertised coast to coast on network television and on cable in most major cities.

So who deserves the credit for this success? Does it

belong to Orville Merillat, an Ohio farm boy and Coast Guard ship's carpenter? That's what most people assume; but there is a lot more to the success of Merillat Industries than Orville Merillat.

Some men succeed without a supportive, capable wife, but I couldn't have done that. I needed Ruth. The Merillat name on a kitchen cabinet doesn't refer to me alone. It refers to a team, both Orville and Ruth. In 1991 we celebrated our fiftieth wedding anniversary. That's a lot of years—a lot of good years. Whenever anyone starts to pat me on the back and tell me how successful I've been, I am quick to let them know that Ruth gets most of the credit for all the good things that have happened these past fifty years.

But more importantly, I needed God. Merillat Industries is the story of what God can do in the life of a willing person. Some men ignore God and succeed anyway, at least by the world's standards. I might have done the same, to some extent. I always worked hard and came up with good ideas, and I am told that such habits can lead to success. But I wouldn't have wanted it that way.

Looking back I can see how God's guiding hand led me along, step by step, despite my own occasional reluctance and rebellion. There were times when my own plans were leading me toward trouble, and God allowed things to happen which steered me back onto His path. He picked me up when I stumbled. He corrected some of my mistakes, prevented others from occurring in the first place, and ignited in me some new ideas that helped Merillat Industries surge ahead. I may not always have recognized God's guiding hand at the time, but I can't help but see it now.

During the past few years Ruth and I have been awarded four honorary doctorates, membership in our industry's "hall of fame," and I have been recognized as "Business Person of the Year" in various state, county, and regional industry organizations. But we are always careful to separate the public figures being recognized from the simple people we really are.

Each honor is a treasure; we don't want to undervalue any of them. And we are truly grateful for the sentiments that have been expressed toward us, but we want to be quick to say that we understand such awards as appreciation for the work God has been able to do in and through us. Ultimately, it is not we who are being honored but God.

God did not choose me from the world's masses and say, "I'm going to give some special attention to Orville Merillat." His guiding hand rests upon all faithful Christians, of whom I am just one of millions. For most people, faithfulness to God doesn't lead to wealth and recognition. Ruth and I have known many godly people who never achieved success as the world measures it, yet they are people who have been an example and an inspiration to us. And they have been just as happy and fulfilled in life as we have been. They, too, have experienced God's guiding hand.

But for Orville and Ruth Merillat, wealth and recognition were part of the package—though for God's benefit, not ours. The success of Merillat Industries enabled us to donate millions of dollars to worthy causes. We have been able to contribute to the education of children through the Lenawee Christian School and various Christian colleges. We have supported missionary work around the world, helped start new churches, contributed to Christian camping, and many other things. God made the funds available through us. We couldn't foresee all of this back when we began Merillat Industries, but God knew exactly where He was leading us. It has been a unique privilege for both of us to be used in that way and to see the hand of God at work in our lives.

The pages that follow tell the story of Orville and Ruth Merillat and of the growth of Merillat Industries. I am pleased that Dr. D. James Kennedy was willing to provide the foreword to this book. He has helped to clarify certain aspects of our story and to focus new attention on aspects of our business—such as the Trust and Share Program—which are suddenly being discovered by business leaders all over America.

As you read our story, please don't overlook the leading character: God. Our desire is to spotlight His central role in our lives and to give Him the credit which too many people give to us. Ruth and I are just two ordinary people who, long before success overtook us, determined that we would follow Jesus Christ wherever He would take us.

It has been an incredible journey, and we are honored to share it with you now. The purpose of this book is to show the potential within each man and woman, and to show that when people work together in love and commitment—as when a husband and wife become one flesh in the Lord and are dedicated to serving Him—miracles still happen.

ONE

The Man in the Sky

I T WAS A beautiful spring day and Papa and his crew were building a new barn. The older children decided to go watch the carpenters work. Mother wasn't feeling well, so she told my sisters to take little Orv—that was me, the baby—and stay out of the way. Alta and Ilva enjoyed "mothering" me, so they gladly complied. They bundled me up and placed me flat on my back in the wagon.

The loud bumpity-bump rhythm of the wheels on the ground made me drowsy. I was just about asleep when the wagon stopped. Suddenly a man burst forth out of the clear blue sky and climbed down on a ladder. The big man scooped me up, fussed over me, and returned me to the wagon. Then, just as suddenly, he climbed back up the ladder and disappeared into the sky once again.

I have many vivid images of times like this when God has burst from heaven to point my life in a certain direction. But there have been other times when my human emotions insisted that God was nowhere near. I knew from His Word, however, that He was always close by, though just out of sight, ready to swoop down from heaven and take me in His powerful, gentle arms.

His hand has never stopped guiding me. Without it, I fear to think how my life might have turned out. My daily prayer is, "Thank You, Lord Jesus."

BUT THE story really begins a few years earlier. May Day, 1916. It was a cool spring morning, I have been told, and the birds were just beginning to sing their wake-up songs when Emma McCollum Merillat held her newborn son for the first time and sighed in relief. She had taken quick inventory of him after the doctor cut the cord, and the loud cry of disapproval told her that this baby would be all right.

"Thank you, Lord," she whispered.

Just eighteen months before, a baby girl had been stillborn. And a year before that, she had buried little three-year-old Ivan. Her heart and empty arms had ached so badly. She had six others to care for, but the pain never let up until she learned that another child was on the way. That other child had now arrived safely.

The baby was cleaned and dressed and presented to the rest of the family, who had been waiting patiently in the kitchen. The children—Mary, Alta, Walter, Vernon, Francis, and Ilva—filed one by one into the bedroom to kiss their mother and welcome their new baby brother.

"His name is Orville D. Merillat," my father declared, and the doctor promptly wrote the name on the birth certificate. There was only time for a brief observance of the occasion, a short pause in the day's routine, then Papa said, "Okay, children, it's time for chores," and the parade marched back out the way they had come.

Such was my arrival.

As soon as the doctor finished his business at the house, he headed back to town. His horse and buggy turned back up the path and out onto the main two-track road. The children tended to their chores, busily rushing around on tiptoe and talking in loud whispers so they wouldn't disturb their mother and sleeping baby brother. The girls handled the housekeeping while Papa and the older boys milked the cows, hauled water, pitched hay, and fed the animals.

As I grew older, I took my place alongside them. Eventually, there were thirteen children in our family. Laura arrived a year after me, and she was followed by Wanetta, Vera, Lavina, Kenny, and Alice. I was right in the middle, with six older siblings and six younger.

Life on the Farm

My father, David Merillat, was a sober man of few words. He had one of the largest farms in our area. While most men tilled about eighty acres, the Merillat farm covered 150 acres of prime Midwestern soil near Wauseon, Ohio. At age thirty-four he asked Emma, then only sixteen, to be his bride.

Keeping body and soul together on the farm took a lot of hard work. Farmers depended on their sons and daughters to keep the "family business" afloat. Children, like everyone else, had several responsibilities, in addition to keeping up with their studies. People were busy about the task of surviving, and there was precious little time for leisure.

Money was also scarce. We used the barter system for most things we needed, trading corn for cornmeal, wheat for flour, oats for rolled oats, cream and eggs for sugar, salt, spices, and other items. Meals consisted mostly of oatmeal or pancakes for breakfast, cornmeal mush for lunch, and sometimes even fried cornmeal mush for supper. Mother canned vegetables and fruit when they were in season, but the mainstay was cornmeal.

Suppers usually featured just the main dish. If someone complained too loudly about what was served for supper, Papa would say, "Go to bed. We will eat again tomorrow." After going to bed hungry a few times, we learned to appreciate whatever Mother put on the table.

I learned to use a walking plow at age ten. I was lucky if I didn't get knocked on my behind a couple times a day. Sometimes, I would hit a stump or stone; the horse would keep going, but the plow would stop and then jerk suddenly forward, sending me sprawling in the dirt. It was a man-sized job, and I was proud of my work.

When a cow got too old, it was fattened up and butchered. That put meat on the table for a while. Since we had no refrigeration in those days, fresh beef had to be eaten quickly or prepared for long-term storage; so Mother would can some of it and make the rest into beef jerky.

Emma Merillat, Orville's mother, in 1945.

Holidays were observed, not celebrated. We couldn't afford expensive gifts or even a fancy holiday meal. Like others, we recognized the holiday for what it was, not for the good time or gain we would receive from it. We didn't put up a Christmas tree, and we certainly didn't have a lot of presents to unwrap. Many times we all shared the same gift, like a wagon, along with some homemade candy and nuts.

During the summer, the flies were terrible. We used what we called "fly chasers"—old flour sacks cut into strips and wrapped around a stick—to chase them out the door. When a new spray called Fly-Tox hit the market, Papa used it to spray the flies in the kitchen and dining room when he got up at 4:30 each morning. After completing the morning chores, he'd come back in and sweep up half a pail full of dead flies!

For several years, kerosene lamps provided our only light. Papa took a lantern out to the barn to do chores, but since there was just one lantern, we did most of our work in the dark. Then one day electricity arrived in rural Wauseon. It was a novelty at first, and if we behaved ourselves and were especially good, Mother would tell one of us, "You can turn the lights on now." The honored child would then walk to the wall and flip the switch. That was quite a treat.

I had another treat during those years: I learned to play baseball. Papa used to say, "I can't figure out why it takes Orv twenty minutes longer to get home from school than the other children." Of course, he knew the reason: I was playing ball. But sometimes Papa liked to let the children think they were pulling the wool over his eyes. My love for baseball didn't get me into very much trouble, as long as I didn't keep the family cow waiting too long to be milked. But when I lost track of time, as boys often do, I would really catch it.

Simple Pleasures

One summer highlight was when Papa took the family to the lake for the day. We would pack a lunch and spend the whole day splashing, eating, and playing. Another highlight was going to the fair. Papa would give us each fifty cents and then drop us off at the entrance to the fairgrounds with the understanding that we were to meet back there at a certain time. We felt rich as kings walking around with all that money.

It is hard to realize now how much that half dollar was worth back then. In those days there was nothing to eat at the fair, just rides and games. And since the main attractions were mostly contests and exhibits, we usually went home with our money unspent.

When sickness struck the family, everyone got it. We

Orville's parents, seated, second and third from left,
with several of his sisters, in 1940.

were quarantined whenever anyone came down with the mumps, measles, chicken pox, diphtheria, whooping cough, or scarlet fever. That meant no school, so we'd do lessons at home to keep up with the others. It seemed that just when quarantine was lifted, someone would come down with something else, and the long convalescence would start all over again.

To earn extra money, my brothers and I dried and sold walnuts and hickory nuts. I also cut wood on "shares." If a neighbor had wood to cut, we would cut it up, and the neighbor would give us half of it, which we would then try to sell. There were still quite a few wild varmints in the area, so trapping also brought in a few dollars. Whatever the need was, the family pulled together to meet it. That was our way of life.

There were no real roads at the time, only two tracks. However, surveyors had laid out space for the roads, and we ended up building our own road in front of our farm. At age twelve, I found myself doing another man-sized job—working on a horse-drawn scoop-scraper, dragging the scooper where the road was to be and dumping it.

Mother was very patient. She had to be. With thirteen children, she was constantly cooking, cleaning, mending, washing, and doing a myriad of other things that went along with being a mother and a farmer's wife.

Eventually, she began having problems with her eyesight and her health, and she required more help from the children to run the household. I helped with various tasks, even washing clothes on the scrub board from time to time.

Every Sunday, Mother and Papa got us dressed, loaded us into the horse-drawn buggy, and headed for the

Mennonite church. More than anything, they wanted to teach their brood to love and obey the Lord, so they did it by example. Liquor was never allowed in the house, and they would not tolerate disrespect or laziness.

Sunday was the day of rest and, except for taking us all to church, even the horses got the day off. Except once, that is.

It had been a hard spring and summer, and one hot Sunday afternoon Papa felt he needed to get caught up, so he hitched the horses to the mower and began working. Suddenly, one of the horses dropped to his knees. When Papa jumped down to see what had happened, the horse fell on its side and died, still in the harness.

I can imagine the shock and loss my Papa must have felt. He decided then and there that God meant business when He said to rest on the Sabbath, and to my knowledge he never again worked a horse on Sunday.

Mother's health continued to deteriorate until she was unable to attend church every Sunday. Papa tried to get us ready all by himself, but the older boys protested so much that he eventually gave up. The girls and the younger children continued to go to Sunday School while my older brothers and I stayed home, thinking church was unnecessary for us. However, our parents never stopped praying that God's guiding hand would protect and lead us.

It was into such a time, such a place, and with such a heritage that God first blessed me.

An April Fool Drop-Out

Tedrow Elementary School was a two-room, two-story building with four grades on the upper floor and four grades on the lower and just two teachers. I spent eight years there.

I was a good student when I applied myself, but that wasn't often. Lessons came easily to me, especially math. I had a gut feeling about what was correct and liked to come up with ballpark figures instead of exact numbers, which I felt took too much time. When forced to do it correctly, I would get bored and start contemplating mischief rather than math. While the teacher was at the blackboard, I'd make noises, scrape my feet, or tease the kids around me.

I worked just hard enough to get by. The fact is, my mischief exasperated the teacher so much that she wanted to expel me. But since it was near the end of my eighth grade year, she would just shake her head and say, "Merillat, no matter what, you're not going to be in this classroom next year."

She was right. I never returned to that classroom, or even to that school. Instead, in 1931, I started ninth grade at Pettisville High School. It was a large building, just two years old, and there were many new students from area grammar schools.

This was during the Great Depression. Times were tough everywhere, but life in rural Ohio was especially hard. The Merillat children wore hand-me-down clothes. What started as a new piece of clothing would be passed from one child to the next until it finally reached the youngest. By then, it was well-worn and covered with patches. And since Mother washed clothes with a scrub board in a large metal tub, the fabric became so thin you could practically see through it.

I got my first new shirt and corduroy pants just before

starting high school. Even though I felt nervous and a little out-of-place, I was proud to be wearing something none of my brothers had ever worn. But after six months of daily wear, those new clothes began falling apart. And neither they nor my high school career would survive April Fools' Day, 1932.

When I arrived at school that morning, a group of boys was joking with each other and pulling April Fool's tricks on other students. The minute they saw me coming, they ran up and tried to pull my pants down to embarrass me. But the worn fabric wouldn't take much horseplay. When they tugged at my trousers, the fabric ripped open, tearing from the fly all the way down the leg.

I was so embarrassed, I didn't know what to do. I ran behind the waste basket and stood there while the others filed into the room. Then, realizing I had to get out of there, I bolted from the room and the building. I walked the five miles across the fields to my home in the total humiliation and shame only a fifteen-year-old-boy at the threshold of manhood can know.

It was the last day I attended school.

In those days, most farm kids quit school at age sixteen, the legal drop-out age, because they were needed at home. Since I was just one month away from my sixteenth birthday, my father took the chance that I wouldn't be forced to come back to school. So he put me to work full-time on the farm.

That year, 1932, saw the repeal of prohibition and the introduction of 3.2 beer. Prior to that time, many people ran their own stills. But Papa was a teetotaler, and I followed his example.

Nevertheless, life was not without its temptations. Francis, my brother who was five years older, was a carouser. He'd go down to the fair at night and hang out with other guys, drinking and carrying on. Since our family was so large, I had to share a room and a bed with Francis. Occasionally, he came home late feeling a bit sick and would have to get to the bedroom window quick. Sometimes he made it, but sometimes he didn't.

I decided then that alcohol was not for me. Like Papa, I would be a teetotaler. No glass or bottle would dictate how I lived. Francis and others teased me now and then, but I stuck to those convictions—not only then, but for the rest of my life.

Except once, that is.

One evening, after playing baseball with the fellows, an older friend, one of the local boys who had his own home, invited us to come over to his house for some cider. But it turned out to be a fairly potent dandelion wine. Everyone knew what it was except me, and I drank some. They all winked at each other as I gulped it down.

Afterwards, we drove to town to see a street film (we didn't have an indoor theater). When I got out of the car, I was dizzy and staggering. Feeling ashamed and not wanting anyone to see me stagger, I leaned against the building throughout the picture.

That lesson convinced me to stay away from liquor. I decided to concentrate harder on my work around the farm. Actually, I didn't mind farming, even though I often worked more than ten hours a day. When I went to bed at night, I was dead tired, and that kept me out of trouble. However, I was generally discontent, convinced deep inside that I was destined for greater things. The more I farmed, the more I realized there was no future in it for me.

But what did I want to do? While I struggled with my emotions and all the fears and hopes of young manhood, I continued working for my father for two more years.

By the time I reached age seventeen, things were not so good at home. Mother's eyes continued to deteriorate. She developed cataracts, which left her almost totally blind and in need of an operation. Her helplessness placed a heavy burden on the family, and we all carried a heavy load. Papa already had more than he could handle, but sometimes it was easier to do a job himself than to argue with the older boys as to who would help.

Church attendance became very irregular. The family suffered spiritually as well as physically, and I strayed from the godly way I had been brought up with; and that led to what may have been the greatest mistake of my life.

Go West, Young Man!

My brother Walter, who worked on the railroad, bought the first radio in the Merillat household. We all hurried to finish our chores so we could sit around the radio listening to "Amos and Andy."

Walter also brought home Zane Grey western magazines, which fueled my discontentment on the farm. Those magazines portrayed the West as a glorious place—the place a young man had to go to succeed. I read those stories and lived them out in my daydreams. The slogan, "Go West,

Young Man, Go West!" whirled in my head. The idea of going West was all I thought about when I was alone.

Months went by. I kept farming, kept reading, kept dreaming, and I kept growing more and more restless. I wanted to go somewhere, be somewhere. Anywhere in the world, anywhere except home, seemed like the place to be. And finally I made a decision. I would go west.

It was an eerie feeling. Nobody gave me advice, and I certainly didn't want to ask God about it, knowing in my heart that He wouldn't approve. Instead, I would go it on my own. With youthful defiance, I devised a not-too-well-thought-out plan.

According to the Zane Grey magazines, a man needed a gun out West because there was so much lawlessness. Since the West was a dangerous place, I decided to take my brother's pistol. But I would also need some transportation. For that, I would buy a motorcycle with the family savings, which was kept in the cookie jar in the kitchen. I figured the sixty dollars in the jar, plus my savings of three dollars and seventy cents, would be plenty.

I wrapped the pistol in some extra clothes. Then, making sure nobody saw me, I walked the quarter-mile to the barn on the far side of our property and hid the bundle in the manger under the hay. I would pick it up later, after getting the motorcycle.

With this secret, I felt powerful, exhilarated, and in control. I woke up early and did my chores, like always. But on this day, I was particularly alert and anxious. Nobody saw me in the kitchen fumbling with the cookie jar. And nobody saw me leave.

The Man in the Sky

April Fools' Day, 1934. Exactly two years before, I had left Pettisville High School in shame, sneaking across the field toward home in my torn jeans. Now, I backtracked across those same fields to Pettisville. This time, I not only took shame with me, I also gave it to my family.

Once I reached Pettisville, I decided to skip the motorcycle and take the trolley to Toledo. That meant leaving the clothes and pistol back at the barn, but I didn't care. I was exhilarated to be out on my own. I was going West! What wonderful adventures I would have! Maybe someday they would write magazine stories about me for everyone to read in those Zane Grey magazines!

By the time my family reported I was missing and the county sheriff began searching for the runaway, I was already in Toledo. I bought a bus ticket to Chicago, not realizing it would have been cheaper to buy a ticket straight to Los Angeles.

I had never seen a big city like Chicago, and I was stunned. There were so many people. Not knowing anyone, I wasn't sure what to do next. The only friendly person I met was the man who wanted to sell me a ticket to St. Louis. I bought one, not knowing that St. Louis was due south, not west. Spur-of-the-moment decisions like that showed how naive I really was.

St. Louis seemed as foreign to me as Chicago, so I didn't even leave the bus station. I bought a ticket to Kansas City, where I bought a ticket to Denver. The same situation repeated itself in Denver, where I finally bought my ticket to Los Angeles.

On the way, we stopped in Reno, Nevada, which was

very exciting and different from anything I had seen. Back on the bus, I gazed in awe at the mountains. They were so grand—nothing at all like Tedrow, Ohio. I was really enjoying myself, not realizing the predicament that awaited me.

The Land of Dreams

After a week-long journey, I finally arrived in Los Angeles, California,—the romantic West, the place of my dreams.

Now what? I had no plans, just three dollars to my name, and no one to welcome me or take me in. I was an outsider in a totally new world, a stranger in a strange land.

I spent the night sleeping on the streets of Los Angeles. A green farm boy from Ohio was an open invitation to pickpockets who knew how to take advantage of newcomers. And they knew all the places someone like me might try to hide his money. By morning, my last three dollars were gone.

This was too much for an innocent seventeen-year-old. One night on the streets of Los Angeles during the Great Depression was enough for me. I thought of the money I had wasted, the pain I had caused my family, and the miles that separated us now. I thought of my mother and father. What could they think of me now? I had sunk as low as I could go, and I could only think of better days back in Ohio. I realized I had to get out of this place as quickly as I could. I had to get back home, somehow. Without a nickel or even a plan, I started walking.

Hitchhiking east from Los Angeles in 1934 was very slow. Only a couple cars an hour came by on that highway, so I mostly walked. If they stopped and gave me a ride, that was okay. If they didn't, that was okay, too. At least I was making some headway. To where, I didn't know. But I was certain I didn't want to go back to Los Angeles.

After traveling for several days under the hot sun and eating vegetables and fruit from along the roadside, I arrived, tired and dirty, in Blythe, California. I had crossed the state to the Colorado river, and beyond me lay a vast and dangerous stretch of desert. Blythe was just five miles from the Arizona border, and it was the last stop at the doorway of the great Mojave desert.

I had come to a moment of destiny: a turning point 2,000 miles from home.

TWO

A Bridge in Blythe

I N EVERYONE'S life there are opportunities to change, turning points where we suddenly realize that we just can't do it alone, no matter how hard we try. Even though we thought we were right, we finally admit that we have made a real mess of things, and we're truly sorry.

Like the Prodigal Son. The Bible tells the story of a rebellious young man who demanded his inheritance and then left home to make his own way in the world. But soon he squandered everything and found himself eating less than the pigs he was hired to feed. Thinking about everything he had left behind on his father's farm, he finally admitted that he'd had it pretty good back there. Even the poorest of his father's servants had it better than he had. He wrestled with his conscience and finally decided to return home and ask his father for a job as a servant.

That loving father, however, wouldn't hear of it. He didn't want his son back as a servant, but as the beloved son he had lost. He greeted the repentant young man with a joyful embrace and brought out new clothes for him. Then he ordered the servants to kill and prepare a fatted calf so they could celebrate with a great feast.

Before he could enjoy that incredible homecoming, however, and before he could even admit to himself that he had blown it, the prodigal had to hit rock bottom. I reached that point on a bridge in Blythe, California.

On that hot, lonely bridge in the tortured summer of 1934, I was a homeless, penniless, hungry teenage boy depending on his own wits and the generosity of strangers. Wandering far from home, a Depression-era prodigal son, I could only dream of fatted calves.

As I walked east from Los Angeles, regret and self-pity engulfed me. I thought about how worried my parents must be, and how they were probably praying for my safe return. My sudden departure no doubt embarrassed them in the community. They had depended on me, and I had let them down.

Having eaten nothing but roadside fruit for several days, I feared starvation. I looked like a filthy, dirty tramp—and I smelled like one, too. Despite exhaustion, I was unable to get much rest sleeping on the ground. And I still had 2,000 miles to go.

How would I ever get home? Hopelessness nearly overwhelmed me. As I trudged up to that deserted bridge, I thought about the prodigal son and I knew exactly how he must have felt.

Although I didn't realize it at the time, I had pretty much come to the end of traffic. Little but hot desert lay ahead of me, and few cars. If I had crossed the bridge and continued east, I might have been stranded in the desolate Mojave desert and perished there. But God heard the cry of my heart.

Angels of Mercy

Looking east, then back west, tired, humiliated, crying in my soul, it seemed as if I heard a still small voice within me saying, "Orville, you have made a mess of your life in just nine short days. Come rest awhile on this bridge railing."

The old bridge was located next to a school yard, and I could see the groundskeeper across the playground mowing the lawn. As he came near the bridge, he noticed me standing there.

"Hello!" he called out.

I looked up with a start, waved, and greeted him in return.

"Where are you from?" the man asked as he came nearer.

"Ohio," I called out.

"What part of Ohio?"

"Wauseon."

He smiled. "I'm from Toledo."

With something in common, we moved closer together and chatted for a while. His name was O'Keefe and he had come west many years before but had never gotten farther than Blythe.

I told him how I'd gone west and was on my way back home. He was amazed that he had stumbled upon someone from back home and was as happy as I was to speak of familiar places.

O'Keefe invited me to his home that evening for dinner with his family. He and his wife had four children, up to age twelve. What a feast I had! After nine days without a regular meal, it seemed like everything—including the fatted calf. I ate until I couldn't hold another bite.

Something told Mr. O'Keefe the fix I was in, and that I needed some help. "I know a place where you can find work, if you want it," he told me. "As far as a place to live, you can stay with us."

He didn't have to wait long for an answer.

That night I took my first bath in nine days—my very first in a real bathtub, not a washtub. It was a treat, indeed. After shampooing, shaving, and putting on some borrowed clothes, I looked half-way respectable.

Lying in bed later that night—a real bed, and how wonderful it felt!—I thought again about what I had run away from: Mother, Father, a loving home. I couldn't imagine what had possessed me to cause my parents so much heartache. I remembered the song Mother used to sing when I was a child, "Oh, where is my wandering boy tonight?" Tears of remorse soaked my pillow, as I began to understand just how blessed I had been. But my bone-weariness and physical and mental exhaustion soon overcame me, and I fell into a deep, restful sleep.

"Breakfast is ready!"

I had just fallen asleep, it seemed, when I heard Mrs.

O'Keefe calling us all to the kitchen. I climbed out of bed, rested and renewed, for yet another feast, this time of bacon, eggs, potatoes, and toast.

After breakfast, Mr. O'Keefe took me to the Paloverde Valley, where he found me a job working in the produce fields cultivating vegetables. Having any job at all in the early 1930s was something to be proud of, and I was glad to have this one so quickly.

I carried a lunch and walked to work every day. Having grown up on a farm, I wasn't afraid of hard work and I felt right at home in those fields.

I was a good worker and didn't complain. In fact, work became the most enjoyable part of my life. After a twelve to sixteen hour day, I would get a good night's sleep and look forward to another twelve to sixteen hours of the same. I might as well enjoy it, I reasoned. So I did.

When I picked up my first wages, I bought some three-cent stamps and sent my first letter home to Mother and Dad, telling them where I was and that I was okay. I knew they would fall on their knees with joy and gratitude when they received it, thanking God that their wayward son was safe.

As a child, I had often made night-time trips to the outhouse, and when I tip-toed past my parents' room I would sometimes see my father and mother on their knees in prayer for our family. I always felt I was intruding on something, but it made me feel good to hear my father mention my name. It taught me more than the best Sunday school class could have.

I knew my parents were still praying for me back in Ohio, and even there in Blythe I could sense God's presence at my side.

Ultimate Realities

Like the prodigal son, I had left a good life at home to make my own way in the world—and I had, in the process, made a mess of my life. It seemed like everything I had planned to do no longer appealed to me.

Having fallen as low as the prodigal, I now had a decent job, good food, and a nice place to stay. But as I lay in bed at night, I couldn't forget the life I had left back in Ohio, or the parents who loved me. All I could think about was going home.

God was already working on that, though I certainly was unaware of it. Even when I followed my own poorly-planned agenda, He had a plan for my life and kept guiding me gently with His strong hands, protecting me from my own mistakes.

Terrible things could have happened to me on the trip west, or on the streets of Depression-era Los Angeles, or on that lonely desert road. But He had kept me safe across 3,000 miles. And He eventually led me to a bridge in Blythe, where, in response to the cry of my prodigal heart, He bridged the chasm in my own heart.

I cannot tell you how large that seemingly chance encounter with Mr. O'Keefe now looms in my heart, after more than fifty years. For God knew, though I didn't at the time, that Mr. O'Keefe would be my ticket home.

The Prodigal's Return

When I was young, one of my morning chores before going off to school was to help Papa husk a few shocks of corn. More than once, as we talked in the barn, he said to me, "Orville, a man's name is his most treasured possession. See to it that you don't bring shame to yours."

Papa followed his own advice. He was well-respected in the community, as well as in his family. Like most men of his day, he wore the pants in the house, and there was no negotiating with him. He was a man of his word who loved God—a role model for his children, and a testimony to his peers.

Then there was Orville. I knew that my parents must be deeply disappointed with me. By running away, I not only heaped shame upon myself, but I stained the Merillat name— a respected name which my father had spent a lifetime honoring. I had not only hurt myself, I had hurt my whole family, especially my father.

I boarded with the O'Keefes for about three months. Then one day Mr. O'Keefe received an urgent telegram. His mother was very ill, and the family asked him to return to Toledo immediately. Without hesitation, the entire family got packed and prepared to leave.

O'Keefe came back to my room and explained the situation. He looked at me for a moment, then said, "For ten dollars you can ride to Ohio with us, if you want."

Ten dollars was a lot of money, but I had been saving up, and I jumped at the chance to return to familiar territory.

"I'm going home," I said without hesitation.

That afternoon everyone piled into the O'Keefes' 1927 Chevrolet pickup truck, along with a lot of confidence that we would make it. Mr. and Mrs. O'Keefe rode in the front seat of the cab with the youngest child, while the three older children joined me in the open box in back. We drove straight through, averaging fifteen miles per hour. The trip was dirty, tiring, and terribly boring. The only highlights were stops for gas and oil, tire problems, and occasional pit stops for the seven passengers.

It was the most uncomfortable trip of my life—but not just because of the traveling conditions. It would not be easy facing my family. My own searing conscience made me squirm just as much as the hard wooden surface in the back of the truck.

Six days after leaving Blythe, we reached West Unity, Ohio. My sister Alta lived there, and that's where I asked to be dropped off. Mr. O'Keefe would have taken me straight home, but I didn't have the courage to face my father in those circumstances. Not yet, anyway. So, shaking hands, I said thank you and goodbye to the man God used to save my life.

I knocked on the door. Alta gasped when she saw me. What a sight I was! After an instant's hesitation, she threw her arms around me. Alta had consoled Mother many times since scalawag Orville had left. But I was her little brother, and her anger gave way to joy knowing how relieved Mother would be to have me home—especially today.

I arrived at my sister's house thinking I had plenty of time before I would have to face my father. But that wasn't the case.

"You need to get cleaned up very quickly," she told me. "Grandfather died, and we need to be at the cemetery for his funeral in just four hours."

After riding cross-country non-stop for six days in the back of an old pickup truck, I was dead tired. I desperately needed a head-to-toe scrubbing, a shave, and a hair trim. But I complied, and with no time for a rest, Alta fitted me with one of her husband's old suits. Then we were off to the cemetery.

Moment of Truth

Not wanting to be noticed right away, I stayed in the back, as inconspicuous as possible. But Alta immediately informed Mother of my arrival. Mother then turned to Papa and whispered, "Orv's here." He didn't look up.

My thoughts raced. I felt sad about the passing of the only grandfather I had ever known. Because of his failing health, he came to live with us when I was about fifteen. I helped him grow mushrooms in the cellar, where it was damp and dark. In those few years before I left home, Grandfather and I became very close. I would miss him, but I was glad I made it back in time for his funeral.

The service ended much too quickly, and it was time to leave. One by one, my brothers and sisters came by to give me a piece of their mind and to welcome me home. They told me to go to Papa, but I was afraid.

Finally, Mary grabbed my arm and led me to where my father stood. It was an awkward moment for both of us. With a big push from the family, we shook hands. No harsh words passed between us, but it was an agonizing experience. I made no apology—not because I wasn't sorry, but because I knew it would have been inappropriate, and unwanted, at this time.

Papa was a proud man who had worked very hard all his life to give his family the best home possible. It had hurt him deeply when I disregarded his authority and ran off the way I did, and he didn't know how to handle this reunion any more than I did.

I knew he was glad I had come home, but I also knew I couldn't undo the hurt I had caused with a few words spoken in a cemetery. To Papa, actions spoke louder than words. Forgiveness and trust had to be earned, and it would take time to repair the damage. I knew that.

As I looked into my father's face, I saw pain and embarrassment in his eyes. I recalled the fatherly advice he had given me while husking corn years before. Right there I vowed, with God's help, that Orville Merillat would never again bring shame to another person.

From Farmer to Carpenter

One time, when I was a child, I overheard my mother telling my father, "I can always depend on Orv to bring me a full bucket of water."

I can't describe how much that meant to me. I treasured Mother's regard for me, and it made me happy to know she appreciated my efforts. After overhearing a compliment like that, I would walk a little straighter and do my very best at anything she asked. After all, I felt I had a reputation to uphold.

Upon returning from California, I set about rebuilding the reputation which my youthful defiance had shattered. As I determined to regain lost favor with my family, I also gained a new outlook on life.

Alta and her husband found a job for me working on

a neighbor's farm. I earned thirty dollars a month, plus room and board.

Again, God's guiding hand was at work. The farmer was the Sunday school superintendent, and he lived the Christian life as an example to me. For the next sixteen months, I again enjoyed farming, not minding the long hours or the back-breaking work. Nevertheless, I saw no future for me on the farm. I still sensed that I was destined for greater things; and just as I had decided before heading west, I knew the farm wasn't the place for me.

Alta's husband occasionally hired me to help with his daily milk route. In those days, each farmer had his own cans and might have anywhere from one to a dozen or so cows. We picked up the full milk cans, took them to the dairy, and then delivered the empties back to the farmer. We had to keep the cans in the proper order on the back of the truck so the farmers would be sure to get their own cans back. My brother-in-law had this rotation down pat, but I didn't. What a mix-up he would face the next morning! And yet he still asked me to make the run with him when he really needed the help.

Back at home, my father needed help more often than usual. The other boys should have been doing the chores, but the work wasn't getting done. So with the family's encouragement, I went back home and helped my father. I quickly fell into the familiar routine: arise at 5:00, help Dad feed the cattle and horses, clean the stables, and then eat breakfast.

After breakfast, I went looking for a job, walking wherever I had to go. Three weeks later, in November of

1936, I landed a job working for a carpenter. At last, I would have the chance to learn a trade!

I worked ten hours each day, six days a week, starting at fifteen cents an hour. It took two hours to get there, and another two hours to get home. After chores, I would fall into bed around 9:00 P.M. But the long hours didn't bother me. This, after all, was the Depression. If I didn't like the hours, I could step aside and someone else would gladly take my place. But I was used to working long hours. And after a sixty-hour week, I had another nine dollars in my pocket—good money back then.

I greatly enjoyed doing something I was good at. I tried hard to be the best workman on the job. I didn't always succeed, but I always tried, and I caught on quickly.

For several months, I walked to a neighbor's house and rode with him to work. Then I decided to buy my first car: a 1930 Wippet, which was one step up from walking. If I drove over thirty-five miles per hour, I had to spend as much time repairing it as I did driving it. So, of necessity, I became a mechanic—grinding valves, tuning spark plugs, and changing the oil and tires.

When Grandfather died, my brother Vernon inherited his carpentry tools. Since Vernon didn't care for carpentry work, I asked him if he would sell the tools to me.

After thinking about it, he replied, "Sure, Orv, they're no use to me. You can have the whole set for twenty-five dollars."

I scraped the money together and took pride in owning the tools. They enabled me to build barns, houses—you name it. To me they were a treasure. I took particular interest in doing specialized work on cabinets, stairs, and fireplaces, and I became good at it. Because of my expertise, I was usually assigned those jobs when we built homes.

My reputation as a skilled craftsman grew quickly, and the boss raised my wages to twenty-five cents an hour. But the best compliment was when a customer asked for me personally to do more work.

By 1937 I was making enough money to afford a better car, and I bought a 1936 Plymouth coupe. It required a lot of polish and care, but I didn't mind. At age twenty-one, I thought I had arrived!

THREE

Becoming a Team

G OD HAS not only kept me on track with His guiding hand, He also placed a wonderful advisor at my side: Ruth. Those who know her agree that, without her, even my best efforts would barely have scratched the surface of what we have accomplished together.

We have always functioned as a team. When the National Association of Evangelicals named Ruth and me "Laypersons of the Year" in 1988, they recognized both of us. That was a great honor for us, especially knowing that the same recognition had in previous years gone to such fine Christians as James Dobson, Chuck Colson, Joni Eareckson Tada, and others. Since Ruth and I have always worked as a team, it was only fitting that we should accept the award as a team.

God knew the type of person I needed for a wife, and I didn't have to go far to find her.

One night, I fell asleep at the wheel while driving home from work. The car ran off a dead-end road, plunged into a ditch, and hit the bank. It knocked me out, and I woke up in the hospital. Even though I had no broken bones, they kept me about a week for observation and then released me to recuperate on my own.

Since my car wasn't badly damaged and I had to take it easy for a while, I decided to go to town and watch the girls go by. I was twenty-two and didn't have a steady girlfriend—not because I wasn't looking, but because chores, work, and tinkering with my car left no time for social life. Finally, I had some time. In those days young men and women met each other walking up and down main street, much the way teens do in the malls today, so that's where I went.

Evelyn Meller, a girl I had dated occasionally, was at the ice cream parlor. Sitting next to her was a beautiful girl I had never seen before, and I immediately fell in love.

I sat there looking at the two of them for a little while, and finally I got brave enough to go sit near them at the counter. In talking to Evelyn, I learned that the other girl was her sister, Ruth.

"Can I give you a ride home?" I asked them.

"Okay," they said.

All the way to their house, I kept glancing at Ruth, wondering if she knew how I felt about her.

Two days later, I mustered enough nerve to call her and ask her for a date. The custom in those days was to have just one date a week, on Friday night. Typically, you went to a movie, ate a dish of ice cream afterward, and then took your date home. So that's what I suggested to Ruth we should do.

To my surprise, she said she couldn't go out with me. "My sister and I made a pact that we wouldn't date each other's boyfriends," she explained.

Thinking fast, I said, "But I'm not really your sister's boyfriend. We only went out once or twice."

After careful consideration, she finally consented.

When I arrived at the Meller farm that Friday night, Ruth wasn't ready. I thought she was just being "fashionably late" . . . until she came into the house from the barn. Wilbur and Edna Meller had four daughters but no sons, so Ruth and her sisters were responsible for the chores. Finally done with her work, Ruth apologized for keeping me waiting and rushed upstairs to get dressed.

We were soon a twosome.

Ruth was a committed Christian. At age seven, with the help of her Sunday school teacher, she committed her life to Jesus Christ. It was a decision she took very seriously. When her mother wasn't able to take her and her three sisters to church, she would ride with a neighbor or walk.

When Ruth and I met, I wasn't a practicing believer, and she knew that. But she also knew I had been raised in a godly home and that I had been taught to respect the things of God.

As time passed, we grew more and more interested in each other, and there were times when we talked about our hopes and dreams; sometimes we talked about marriage. But Ruth wanted things to be done properly. She was still in high school and knew that marriage was a long way off, but that didn't stop us from dreaming and planning a future together. I had never been happier.

In 1939 Ruth graduated from high school, and I popped the question, thinking it was time. To my surprise, Ruth said she wanted to wait until she was twenty before getting married.

"When's that?" I asked.

"January 18, 1941."

"Two years?" I asked. "That's an eternity."

But Ruth was determined to do it that way.

She enrolled in a beauty college in Toledo, and we continued dating. Ruth later commented on this experience, saying, "It took me two years to realize I wasn't cut out to be a hairdresser. I didn't really have the creativity necessary to come up with the best hairstyles for my customers. I should have studied something I had a knack for—like bookkeeping, which is what I ended up doing for many years!"

During the winter months when there was no carpentry work, I drove a truck with my brother to earn money. We traveled to Boston, New York, and Chicago. Being on the road so much, I only had time to see Ruth briefly between runs.

Trying to sustain a long-distance relationship wore thin on both of us, and Ruth finally gave me an ultimatum: either quit the trucking job or stop dating her.

"I'll never have a better reason to quit," I told her. And that's just what I did. I drove into town that day and told my brother I was through.

Becoming a Team

And Two Become One

We continued our courtship during those two long years. Finally January 18, 1941, arrived, and Ruth turned twenty. The next day she invited the pastor to Sunday dinner and invited me to dinner forever.

We were married January 19, 1941.

We honeymooned for a week, and the future appeared to be spread with roses. My boss, a wise man, figured marriage would help settle me down, so he gave me a raise. Instead of twenty-five cents an hour, I was suddenly getting forty cents an hour.

My father, who was getting on in years, couldn't keep the farm going by himself. Since my California adventure I had made real progress and had finally become a son he could be proud of. So, in March of that year, he asked me, "Son, if I bought some new farm equipment, would you work the farm?"

It had been four years since my return from California. I had worked hard to regain my father's respect, and his offer to bring me into the family business was a milestone. I felt forgiven at last.

But I wasn't alone anymore. "Dad," I answered, "there are two of us now. I will have to ask Ruth."

Growing up on the farm had been hard for Ruth. Her father was very difficult to work for, and he drove the girls as if they were men. They did chores before and after school, and they also worked in the fields during the summer. So it was no surprise when she told me, "You're doing pretty well at carpentry, Orv. I'd rather we stay with that."

Her answer relieved me. One reason I ran off to

California was because of my conviction that farming held no future for me. I was pleased to learn that Ruth shared the same attitude toward farming. So I turned down Dad's offer. My older brother Vernon was waiting to take Dad's offer, so I didn't have to feel bad about declining.

From that moment I felt a new sense of independence. At last I was free to be the best carpenter I could be, free from the family farm, and free to face the future—whatever it might bring.

Ruth and I rented our first home for five dollars a month in Tedrow, just about a mile from my parents' farm. The house had a kitchen and a bedroom, to which we added a little furniture. Then we bought our first new car: a 1941 Chevrolet Special Deluxe, for which we paid the grand sum of eight hundred and twenty-seven dollars. Before long, we moved to a new place. This time, our rent went up to thirty-five dollars a month.

Making progress as a skilled craftsman, I began working for a contractor across the border in Michigan, in a small town called Adrian. My wages almost doubled, increasing to seventy-five cents an hour. I helped build gas stations, houses, and other structures.

One of my neighbors in Tedrow worked there also. Together, we rode the thirty miles to and from work, taking a different route each day so we could get to know the area better. Eventually, being on the road so much grew tiresome, so Ruth and I decided to rent a house in Adrian.

Now we were paying sixty-five dollars a month rent, in a new town and a new state, which, for the rest of our lives, we would call "home."

Committed to Uncle Sam and God

Even though I had not yet surrendered my life to God, He was working in my life. I was happy to be busy doing what I wanted to do. The world presented many alluring challenges, but somehow I steered clear of many of the pitfalls of sin. And though I was blind to it at the time, God was preparing me for a lifetime of service to Him.

The greater successes of our lives together lay well ahead of us, beyond our imaginations at the time, but Ruth and I already had many reasons to thank God. He had led me to a vocation I loved, and He granted me the skill to excel at it. He had given us good health and sound minds. And He had given me a wonderful life partner.

Everything was going great. And then came World War II.

December 7, 1941, changed the plans and lives of many people around the world. Less than a year after our wedding, the Japanese bombed Pearl Harbor. I continued working for the Adrian contractor for about six months after the attack. Then, having heard about the big money you could make in the defense factories, I went to Detroit and took a job at Continental Motors. It paid one dollar an hour.

Ruth moved with me, and we rented a house in Detroit for ninety-five a month. But before long, due to the escalation of the war and political climate of the day, I realized that Uncle Sam was on my trail.

Sooner or later I would have to enter the military, but I wanted to choose which branch. So rather than wait for the draft, my budding entrepreneurial spirit took charge. I went to the Federal building in downtown Detroit, where recruiters from all branches of the armed services had stations.

Like most men of the day, I thought I wanted to be a fighter pilot, but in reality I wasn't sure what I wanted. So I went in the first door I came to: the Navy.

The recruiting officer looked over my credentials, which weren't very impressive as far as education goes, but he noticed my carpentry experience.

"I believe I can get you a second-class carpenter's rating," he said. "That would pay eighty-six dollars a month."

That sounded pretty good. The Army was paying just fifty-four dollars a month, and carpenter second class was a good five steps up the rank ladder.

Okay, I thought, if the Navy pays that much, maybe another branch can do better. So I went to the next door, which was the Coast Guard. They gave me a carpenter's test.

"I'm sure I can get you a first-class carpenter's rating," the recruiter urged. "It pays ninety-six dollars a month."

I thought a moment. The next door was the Army, which I had already ruled out, and beyond that was the Marines Corps, which didn't appeal to me—even if they did have the best-looking uniforms.

So the Coast Guard won, and on July 20, 1942, I became the property of Uncle Sam.

After three weeks of boot camp in Chicago, I was shipped to Alameda, California, just across the bay from San Francisco. Ruth moved there with me into an off-base apartment, and she spent the next fifteen months repairing war planes at the Alameda Coast Guard Base. Ruth donned coveralls and mask and learned to use a drill and riveter, thus becoming one of the many women with the nickname, "Rosie the Riveter."

My first assignment was to build an obstacle course. I had never heard of such a thing, and I certainly didn't know how to build one. But with the help of another young carpenter—a fellow who knew as much about such things as I did—we came up with what we called an obstacle course.

About the time Ruth and I were settling into a routine, we received news that my father had died. I arranged for a short leave, and Ruth and I traveled back to Ohio for the funeral.

Getting Our House in Order

Being a private man, Dad disdained immodest hospital garb and he was embarrassment to be waited on when he was sick. So he chose to live with pain, putting off a much-needed operation. By the time he agreed to the procedure, his body had suffered too much damage. He didn't recover.

Like the rest of the family, I didn't know of my father's illness and hadn't expected him to be taken so soon. In fact, I just assumed he would always be there. His death came as a tremendous blow. It was a tearful parting, but I was so thankful that he had released me from the guilt I felt for running away. Still, I didn't recognize the importance of our relationship until it was too late to tell him how much I loved him. I hoped he knew.

Five years later, my mother died. Her health deteriorated steadily since an operation to remove a goiter. Some of the family thought too much had been removed.

Chief Carpenter's Mate Orville Merillat at Riverside Park
in Adrian, Michigan, in 1945.

Orville and Ruth in 1945.

Actually, her body was just worn-out. Giving birth to so many children while in generally poor health had taken its toll. So in the spring of 1946, Emma Merillat went home to be with her Lord, her husband, and the babies who had gone before.

In between those two funerals, millions of men fought, and millions died, in the worst war this world has ever known. But before I eventually joined the Fleet in the South Pacific and took my place in the war effort, there was business to take care of in California.

Back in Alameda, I grew restless. The base had another first-class carpenter ahead of me, so I didn't have much hope of a promotion. I decided I had to get out of there. After considering the options, I applied for Officers Training School at the Coast Guard Academy in New London, Connecticut. With Ruth's encouragement, and with the help of a professor at the camp, I spent a month studying hard for the entrance exam—and I passed!

Before reporting to New London, I had a week of leave, so we used that time to move Ruth back to Adrian to live with her mother.

Ruth worried about me. Even in training there were serious, sometimes fatal, accidents. And with a war raging on both sides of the world, Ruth prayed every day that God would keep me safe. Every day, she watched in silent dread as Western Union messengers pedaled their bicycles down the street, delivering telegrams to neighbors informing them of the death of a loved one.

Knowing there was a high likelihood that I would be going overseas soon, she thought about the dangers ahead of me. As she realized that she might never see me again, a sense of urgency came over her. If Orville were killed, she thought, would he go to heaven? She wasn't sure, and she didn't want to take any more chances.

Ruth had already been through her moment of decision. In the early years of our marriage, the Holy Spirit spoke to her about her commitment. She realized she was holding onto a little of the world. After some struggles, she committed her life fully to Jesus Christ. Nothing the world offered could compare to the peace and joy that came into her heart.

After that, Ruth began experiencing real spiritual growth. She learned to rely on the promises God gives in the Bible, promises such as:

> "Trust in the LORD with all your heart and lean not on your own understanding; in all your ways acknowledge him, and he will make your paths straight" (Proverbs 3:5–6).

> "God is our refuge and strength, an ever present help in trouble" (Psalm 46:1).

> "Every word of God is flawless; he is a shield to those who take refuge in Him" (Proverbs 30:5).

> "Cast your cares on the LORD and he will sustain you" (Psalm 55:22).

As she trusted the Lord more and more, her faith grew stronger. So when she realized that I had probably never made a personal confession of faith in Jesus Christ, and that I might die without Him, she decided to put me into God's hands—immediately!

On our second day back in Adrian, Ruth suggested that we go to the revival services being held at the former United Brethren Church in Adrian. The speaker was Andrew Rupp, a boy I had known when we were growing up. Later he became a bishop and an evangelist in the Mennonite church.

We went to church that night and heard a message called "Quench Not the Holy Spirit." As the meeting progressed, I felt a strange urge to run. Deep in my heart I knew I had been quenching the Holy Spirit in my own life for years, pushing Him aside while I ran my life the way I wanted to. The preacher's words made me restless.

The altar call came and went, and I remained glued to my seat. I was relieved when Andy finally gave the benediction. I planned to slip out the back door without being noticed. But when I reached the back door, Andy was already there. How he got to the back of the church before I did, I'll never know. But there he was.

Andy reached out and took my hand, looked into my startled eyes, and said, "Orv, quench not the Holy Spirit."

I realized that God had been dealing with me throughout the service. At that moment, my heart melted, and I said, "Yes, Lord."

As the hymn "I Surrender All" was being played and people were preparing to leave, I found my way back down the aisle to the altar, and there, through tears of remorse and joy, I prayed with Andy, committing my life to Jesus Christ.

Life is full of decisions, but the one I made that day—to step down from the throne of my life and ask God to sit there in my place—was the most important of my life.

Fifty years have passed since that day, and I have never once regretted that decision.

The date was November 28, 1943. In the outside world, war raged across Europe, the Orient, and the Pacific. I would soon take my place in that turmoil, but that night in Adrian, kneeling at the altar and praying with Andy, a sweet peace flooded my soul.

Ship's Carpenter

Forgiveness is an awesome thing. It releases people to attain their full potential. There at that altar in Adrian, I unloaded all of the inhibiting guilt I had once carried, guilt from running away from home and guilt for running from God. Now, with my whole heart, I wanted to live in a way that would please Jesus Christ.

Having finally committed my life to serve Him, I could see more clearly how His guiding hand had been leading me faithfully along. Many times He had kept me from getting into trouble, and when I did get into trouble, He had bailed me out.

Before, I didn't trust God to direct my life. Now, I did—even though He would soon take me into the heart of the Pacific War.

I reported to the Coast Guard Academy in New London in December 1943. The course lasted ninety days, thus the term "Ninety Day Wonder." After completing the course, most wondered if they would amount to anything.

The rigorous conditions and spit-and-polish atmosphere at the training school were a whole new way of life. The discipline was unbelievably strict, but I quickly caught on.

After a week, this farm boy knew what fork to pick up first and what to use it on. Saluting all officers in the proper manner became routine after a few lectures on military procedure. Having not completed high school, I had a difficult time academically, but I persevered. Things seemed to be going okay. I even began to enjoy it.

Until the fifty-second day.

On that morning my name, along with the names of half my classmates, was posted on the bulletin board. I had flunked out and would be reassigned. Since the war in the Pacific was going better than expected, the Coast Guard didn't need to take as many officers as were being trained, so they dismissed those who were academically borderline.

The discharging officer who processed the reassignments looked me straight in the eye and said, "Merillat, what were you doing here?" The remark stung, but I couldn't blame him. Being sharper than most, he had spotted my lack of education. Today, I say it's a wonder I made it to Officer Training School in the first place!

But I regret none of it. It was a stimulating and broadening experience, and it opened my eyes to things I might otherwise never have thought of.

After I packed all my gear, the Coast Guard sent me back to California, this time to the San Diego naval base, for further reassignment. Within a matter of days, I received my new orders: I was to report aboard the USS America, the United States counterpart to the Queen Mary. I was bound for Noumea, New Caledonia.

The trip to that remote South Pacific island lasted fourteen miserable days, during which we never saw land.

The 13,000 GIs confined to the ship became quite a problem. There were outbreaks of violence as well as seasickness, homesickness, and everything you can imagine. It was a joy to see and feel land underfoot again.

Since I was in the Coast Guard, a branch of service normally assigned to defend North American waters, you might think I was sheltered from the war. That wasn't the case at all. During wartime, the Coast Guard comes under the Navy's authority, and my shipmates and I were treated like Navy personnel and got the same assignments.

War at Sea

At Noumea, I was transferred to a flotilla of Landing Ship Tanks (LST) in New Guinea. Over half of the ships in the flotilla were Coast Guard vessels, the others were Navy. The LSTs were designed to land tanks and troops on beaches. They hurtled through choppy, often crushing surf under enemy fire, with the objective of putting their off-loading ramp down on dry land. Sometimes it worked, sometimes it didn't. On more than one occasion we let down the ramp in the water, and tanks and men and heavy equipment had to slog through several feet of water to get to shore. There were also times, especially in the D-Day landings in Europe and at places like Guadalcanal, Iwo Jima, or Luzon, when either the surf or the enemy fire was too heavy, and many did not make it to shore alive.

I spent the next eighteen months aboard LST-202, taking charge of structural repair and maintenance. My title was "Ship's Carpenter," which is ironic because there wasn't a stick of wood on the ship. Instead, I worked with metal, learning from two second-class firemen working under me how to weld and cut iron.

Our flotilla island-hopped from New Guinea to the Philippines. Along the way, we made eleven "D-day" type landings on islands occupied by Japanese.

Several times, we had trouble backing off from the beach after unloading our men and cargo. When that happened, we had to transfer ballast to help lift the bow free of the suction of the mud. One time our captain ordered the entire crew of 125 men to the fantail. The shift of weight did the trick, and we eased away from the beach and back out to our mother ship.

Time passed rapidly because there was always something new going on. The hectic tour of duty kept me too busy to be scared, and too tired to stay awake off-duty worrying about it.

Then came the invasion of the Philippines. When the Japanese invaders forced General Douglas MacArthur to leave the Philippines, he vowed to return. Several years later, toward the end of World War II, I had the privilege of being in the flotilla which saw MacArthur wade ashore and announce his return.

LST-202 made several more runs after that event. Once we nearly capsized in a hurricane. We raced for cover and took shelter in the calm waters on the leeward side of Corregidor, a prison island which probably had never before brought relief to anyone.

But relief was imminent for all of us, and when it came, it was awesome. On August 5, 1945, a B-29 named The Enola Gay dropped an atomic bomb on Hiroshima. That

Orville, on board LST 202, off the coast of New Guinea in 1944.

historic experiment assured everyone that war would soon end.

That same day I set foot once again on American soil. Words cannot describe how great it felt to be home, or the joy of holding Ruth in my arms again. After twenty months of censored letters, I could finally tell her exactly what I had done and what I had experienced overseas.

I had been promoted to Chief Carpenter while on LST-202. After returning to the States, the Coast Guard reassigned me to Alameda with the recommendation that I be promoted to Warrant Officer—if I wanted to stay on, that is. But I didn't. I had other plans. So, instead, they sent me to Detroit to be discharged.

In my letters home to Ruth, I had frequently outlined plans for our future. My dream was to start a cabinet shop of my own.

FOUR

A Business of My Own

W HILE STILL overseas, I wrote to Rev. Peter, the pastor of the United Brethren Church back in Adrian, and told him I wanted to join the church. He mailed me the membership questionnaire, and I sent back the answers. I eventually completed the membership course by mail, and the congregation accepted me into their fellowship. When I learned of my acceptance, I joked to Ruth, "They must have gotten a little careless!"

The Coast Guard formally discharged me on Saturday, October 20, 1945. The next day, Ruth and I went to church. It was a pleasure to know that when we went there, I came as a member.

If anything in my life has the clear evidence of God's hand in it, it is the fact that the sermon my first day back was on Malachi 3:10. I listened intently to the words of that text:

> "Bring ye all the tithes into the storehouse, that there may be meat in mine house, and prove me now herewith, saith the Lord of hosts, if I will not open you the windows of heaven, and pour you out a blessing, that there shall not be room enough to receive it" (KJV).

I was profoundly struck by this message. If the Bible was the true Word of God, as I knew it to be, and if this was the command of God given to Malachi, the last of the Old Testament prophets, then it should be obeyed. I was struck by the way Rev. Peter explained God's reasonable plea, "prove me now herewith."

God was saying, "Check it out. If you want to see the hand of God in your life, this is how you can do it!" God's promise seemed too good to be true. After church, Ruth and I talked about the sermon and God's wonderful challenge, and we decided to take it.

On that day Malachi 3:10 became my life verse. Ruth and I diligently practiced tithing, giving one-tenth of our earnings back to God, and before our eyes, the promise of Malachi 3:10 was fulfilled and multiplied every year.

"You can't out-give God," some people say, and it's true. In the years ahead, as our business grew, Ruth and I were able to give millions of dollars to Christian causes—schools, churches, missions, and other things. But no matter how much we gave, God seemed to say, "I can do better than that." And He would crack the floodgates of heaven a bit more and deluge us with even greater blessings.

This principle applied just as much in the early years when we started the company from scratch. If we're faithful in little things, the Bible says, we'll be given more. Many people never learn that lesson. They think, "If I had a lot of money, I would give some to God." But you don't need a lot of money to be faithful. You just need a little bit—or even nothing at all.

And that's about where Merillat Industries began: with nothing at all.

Back in Adrian, Ruth had again been doing her part for the war effort by working in a defense factory. She quit her job just before I got home and joked to me, "If you're going to hang around here, you'll have to go to work."

Which I did two days after my discharge. On Monday morning, October 22, I headed off to North Main Street in Adrian and began working in a cabinet shop started by a man I knew from Tedrow. I warned him that I would quit to start my own shop on April 1. He hired me with that understanding, not taking me seriously.

But I was quite serious. So serious, in fact, that I had ordered the machinery before leaving the service.

Every month while serving overseas, I had sent one hundred and fifty dollars home to Ruth and kept just one dollar for myself. Since I didn't drink, smoke, or gamble, and since the Coast Guard was taking care of my room and board and itinerary, I didn't need much spending money. With Ruth adding in her own paycheck, I felt confident that we would have enough money to buy machinery for

Becoming a family. Orville and Ruth
with newborn son, Richard, 1946.

our own cabinet shop when I returned, so I went ahead and ordered it.

Another New Beginning

On April 1, 1946, I quit my job and began building my own shop. April Fools' Day had twice made a fool of me—first, when I quit school, and again when I ran off to California. But having finally conquered the "fool" within, I decided to make it a day of promise and new beginnings.

We sold our old car to a relative and used the money to order a new pickup for the business. GIs supposedly got priority when ordering vehicles, but ours came three months late. In the meantime, we walked everywhere—to church, to the store, to the lumberyard, to the block plant, and to the building site.

By the time summer arrived, we were waiting for three very important things: our pickup, our machinery . . . and our first child.

As it turned out, the child arrived first, on June 20, 1946. On that day Ruth and I became parents to a precious baby boy, Richard. The doctor brought the infant to the waiting room for father and son's first meeting. I was completely disarmed by the emotions I felt.

"Isn't he a cute little fellow?" said the doctor, displaying the newborn.

I could barely squeak out my agreement.

Our joy knew no bounds as we thanked God for our healthy little son and began this new phase of life together. Realizing our awesome responsibility as parents, we claimed another Scripture verse, Proverbs 22:6: "Train a child in the way he should go, and when he is old he will not turn from it." Those words became our guideline for loving and training our son.

The next arrival was the pickup, about a week later, and I proudly drove it all around town. It was our first advertising for Merillat cabinets, and I wanted everybody to see it. That night, when it was too dark to see the truck any more, I parked it in the lot of the Kroger market next door. Bright and early the next morning, I looked out our apartment and there it sat . . . on cement blocks! Someone had stolen the tires of my brand new truck!

Orville and Ruth in front of the first home they owned, 1949.
Orville built the house himself out of cement block and, of course,
did all the carpentry as well.

It was about six weeks later, in August, when the call came that the machinery was in. There was only one problem: we didn't have any money to pay for it. In March, we had $8,250 in the bank, which was a great deal of money in those days. But between living expenses, paying for the new pickup, and the cost of building our shop, the money was all used up.

I explained my predicament to the machinery dealer. He must have thought I would be a good risk, because he decided to take a chance on me. He offered me a deal.

"Take the machinery and set it up," he told me. "Another young man wants to start a window manufacturing plant, but he needs parts. If you cut the parts, I'll supply the lumber, and then you can pay for the equipment as you go."

God was preparing the way for me, once again taking care of things that were beyond my control. He secured my machinery when I couldn't pay for it, and in the process threw in my first long-term customer. It seemed that God wanted this new shop to get off the ground as much as I did.

Maybe more so.

"If It's Made of Wood, I Can Do It"

Merillat Woodworking Company opened for business on September 2, 1946, at 320 Springbrook in Adrian.

I was one proud GI! God had blessed me with a 2,400-square-foot building, new machinery, tools, a truckload of lumber, regular business, and a son at home with Ruth. What more could a man want?

Things started slowly, without much work at first, but I felt confident that the work would come. I applied my "can do" attitude to any job a customer brought to me. I would assure them, "If it's made of wood, I can do it."

When business was slow, I worked on our new house, located just south of the shop. I built it out of cement block and, of course, I did all the carpentry work myself. It was completed in 1947.

For the first three weeks, I handled all the bookkeeping. But I never liked record-keeping. I preferred ball-park numbers, and while that might work in the workshop, it meant chaos for our ledger books. Before long the bills piled up and creditors began calling, wanting to know when I was going to pay them. I would pull out their bill, place it on top, and tell them it was on the top of the pile to be paid. It wasn't a very good system. Usually, that same bill would end up back on the bottom again before any money came in to pay it.

One day Ruth came into the office.

"Where's your desk?" she asked.

"It's under that pile of papers!" I replied.

We hired George Schippers, an accountant, to help the fledgling business. Ruth learned bookkeeping from him, and she had quite a knack for it. She took charge of the books so I could concentrate on the production end of things. After the first six months of operation, the books were in perfect order, with all bills paid.

Ruth's knowledge and expertise grew with the business. She handled payroll, invoicing, accounts payable and receivable, reconciliations, monthly statements—and she actually enjoyed every bit of it. As it turned out, she is a natural businesswoman, and I wouldn't have wanted to run a company without her at my side.

When I had questions, I went to her for answers. She shared her bookkeeping skills with a half dozen people, and at the same time served as mother, doctor, cook, homemaker, and lover. Not to mention all of her church work, such as singing in the choir and helping in junior church.

Ruth handled all of the bookkeeping the first five or six years. But as the business grew, she turned those jobs over to other people. Fortunately, the Lord sent us very good people who deserve a lot of credit for the company's success.

But Ruth's contribution to the business wasn't just bookkeeping, especially in those early years. Many evenings and Saturdays found her out in the shop working with me. She helped me saw lumber, and she worked with the planer, sander, and other machines.

Orville and Ruth at Merillat headquarters, 1961.

Ruth was always willing to take second place, giving the credit to others. But most of what we have achieved in our lives can be credited to her, though she would be the first to deny it. God greatly blessed me by providing this lovely woman to be my companion and wife.

Our combined efforts gave the business a boost when we needed it most. Ruth and I would make plans for reaching more customers and building more and better products, and we could see those plans take shape before our eyes. We wanted to keep expanding. Doing so would provide jobs for more people and also enable more customers to have the best cabinets for the dollar. Our goal was always to benefit other people.

Building with a Boom

Thanks to the post-war building boom, construction picked up everywhere. Schools were being built in the area, and I produced the trim for the doors, windows, and whatever else the customer wanted. A few opportunities to do kitchens came along, as well.

Whenever I went out to bid on a kitchen job, I took a 17- by 23-inch pad and a T-square to design a layout and take special notes. I usually went after work and stayed up well into the night drawing kitchen designs for customers to see and approve.

I used good old-fashioned "gut feelings" when bidding on commercial jobs. With no prior experience, I would bid low and work long hours to get the job done. Gradually, my expertise grew, and I enjoyed the challenges that each commercial job presented. I built showcases, fireplace mantles, stairs, windows, laminated beams, and house doors. I just kept saying, "If it's made of wood, I can do it."

Little by little, however, cabinets became my main line of work. I found myself out every night quoting bids or collecting for a job well done. In those days, I charged $3.50 per cubic foot installed. When it reached the point where we were getting 90 percent of the bids we quoted, we decided to raise our prices—and even then we lost very few bids. A few times customers didn't pay me for cabinets I built; but I can honestly say I never got paid for cabinets I didn't build.

In 1948 I started a building company with a co-worker who was also a boyhood friend. We bought ten acres of land and, over the next several years, built forty houses in an area known as McKenzie Court. We also built a few houses on other sites. We were always on the lookout for new house plans, and we designed some of them ourselves. My partner handled the carpentry, while I produced the cabinets and trim.

After a few years, word got around that Merillat Woodworking Company built quality kitchen cabinets. That reputation reached a prefab home manufacturer in Toledo, and after some discussion they asked me to build cabinets for all of their homes.

This was our first job outside of the Adrian area. I knew I couldn't handle the job myself, but I could hire and train more employees. Training people was nothing new to me; I had trained many while in the service. So I rented more space outside the shop and got to work. Six months later, a second prefab home manufacturer approached me about building cabinets. Over the next three years, it was a real challenge to supply those manufacturers with the number of cabinets they needed.

We had hardly finished the designs for our line of cabinets when we were contacted by a distributor in Chicago who wanted to sell our products. All of a sudden, business was booming. But as we took stock of our situation, we realized that the business was growing almost faster than we could handle it. We eventually dropped all custom work and focused almost entirely on the ever-growing demand for kitchen cabinets.

In 1953 we started building a new plant at the edge of town and moved into it in 1954. It was a 15,000 square-foot building, especially designed and equipped for our manufacturing systems, and it seemed huge in comparison with the original 2,400 square-foot shop.

As business kept expanding, we took on more distributors and employees. A year later, our new facility was bursting at the seams, so we built yet another addition. Over the years, we built nine additions to that plant. Today, that same factory covers 400,000 square feet!

Better Ways to Build Cabinets

One day when I was still working for other people, the contractor walked over while I was doing the trim on a house door. I had become pretty skilled at woodworking and had my own way of doing things. I didn't appreciate people second-guessing my work. But the contractor had his own way, too. In his booming voice, he tried to tell me how the door ought to be done.

A Business of My Own

Finally, after seeing that my way was better, he snorted, "Oh, do it the way you want. You will anyhow!"

Of course, he was right. I would. And I did.

Merillat Industries didn't become the country's largest cabinet maker because we made cabinets the same way everyone else did. It's because we learned to make them better. And that meant doing some things differently from the rest of the pack.

Thomas Edison once said, "There is a simpler way to do everything. Find it." Even though I did not complete high school, I never lacked ideas. I searched relentlessly for simpler and better ways of doing things, and when God blessed me with a good idea, I would try it out and put it to use. He blessed me with some good ones over the years. And thanks to a certain built-in "can do" spirit, I found several simpler ways to improve the art of cabinet-making.

In 1957 I discovered an easier way to guide a drawer. This saved fifty cents on the cost of the drawer. Suddenly, quality began to cost less.

In 1960 an idea came while I doodled on a napkin. Wouldn't it be nice if cabinet doors would close by themselves? I thought. I sketched a self-closing hinge on the napkin and experimented with that pattern. I made a prototype in the shop and discovered that the new hinge eliminated the need for a catch on the cabinet door as well as the door pull. Again, this would offer another huge savings for the customer.

I patented that idea in 1962, and in 1963 I started a new company—Cardinal of Adrian—to manufacture the hinge. Merillat Woodworking now produced the country's only self-closing cabinet doors.

Those innovative ideas greatly improved our ability to serve our customers: the customers were getting better cabinets at lower prices than before. When you do that, you shouldn't be surprised when your market share increases. If you put money in the pockets of your customers, they'll take care of you.

Trusting and Sharing

I'm also proud of the ideas that improved life for the people who make those products and who deserve much of the credit for the company's success—the employees. Wanting the company to be the best it could be, I considered ways to motivate employees to increase production and quality,

Ruth at work at the Merillat corporate offices, 1984.

while also reducing the cost for the customer. With that in mind, we introduced the Trust and Share Program.

Part of this plan involved profit-sharing. We split the savings from the labor portion of increased production. The employees received half of the increased savings, and the company retained half to invest in new plants and equipment.

As we put the plan into action, we counted the number of cabinets produced in one complete work day— that is, from a half hour before quitting time one day to the same time the next day. The last half hour of the day was spent tabulating the day's production report.

In calculating our daily production, employees included only the saleable cabinets. Rejected cabinets could be

Orville and Ruth pose in front of cabinets
made in a Merillat plant.

counted only after being repaired and made marketable. If repair wasn't possible, the cabinet was scrapped, which meant the employees lost part of the labor profit, since they had spent time producing something which we couldn't sell. Consequently, every employee doubled as an inspector.

Before long, peer pressure kept everyone working hard to produce quality cabinets. A marketable cabinet, after all, benefited the entire work force. We told the employees what their production savings was each day, and we paid them for it promptly every week. Within three weeks after we implemented this plan, the entire work force supported the program, and business improved immediately.

A successful fishing trip on Lake Michigan.

Since my co-workers were responsible for much of our success, they needed to share the benefits of that success. This profit-sharing plan was one way to do that. In addition, we trusted our employees. In fact, we came up with the motto, "Trust and be Trustworthy."

We eliminated time clocks and put everyone on salary at the new plants we eventually started. Of all our facilities, only the Adrian plant chose to unionize and stay with the time clock system. We paid workers for forty hours of work each week, whether or not they were present all forty hours. Excessive abuse, we warned, would be grounds for dismissal. We knew there would be times when the car

On their way to visit a Merillat plant on the company plane.

wouldn't start or a child was sick, but those were the exceptions. When employees were late or absent, we trusted them to give us an honest explanation.

People might think workers would take advantage of systems like these, but the absenteeism in our plants dropped to half of the national average. People wanted to be trusted, and when we gave them the chance to be trusted, they performed better—not only living up to our expectations, but exceeding them. I believed in our workers, and they responded.

"A man is known by the company he keeps, and a company is known by the men it keeps." If you take care of your employees, you'll keep them longer. I have never been disappointed with the results of operating with this philosophy.

This same principle works at all levels of the organization. Because the administrative tasks of the growing company consumed so much of my time, I began surrounding myself with quality people to assume many of the responsibilities Ruth and I had once done by ourselves. That freed me to apply my expertise in the factory. The executives and administrative people played a crucial role in the company's success. I believe God sent them.

Just as God's guiding hand kept me out of the ditches and potholes I would surely have wandered into on my own, His loving eye watched over the company and its phenomenal growth. Ruth and I worked hard through all those years and remained faithful to Jesus Christ, and today I can assure you that the real credit for our success belongs to God and His faithfulness to us. We recognized it then, and we recognize it now.

FIVE

Growing Beyond Adrian

I TELL people in the business world, "Your competitor is your best friend. He will influence you to try new and better things."

It has been true in my business life, but it has also been true in my personal life.

When we were growing up, my brother Francis thought it was his job to keep me in line. And since he was five years older, he usually had the advantage on me.

But one day a fellow who was a pretty good boxer helped put up a ring not far from our place, and I took lessons from him. After six months, I was pretty good with the gloves. In fact, at fifteen, I felt invincible.

Francis couldn't bear the idea that his little brother was so cocky and actually thought he could beat him. So he decided it was time to teach me a lesson. It was going to be a showdown, his dukes against mine. To keep things on the up and up, he asked Mother to witness the match so nobody would doubt who was the better fighter.

The bell rang and we went at each other. We jabbed and poked and danced around a lot the way we had been taught, and I suppose we looked pretty silly. There was a lot of laughter. But after taking a couple of solid licks from my big brother, I started to warm up. He dazed me a bit, but just as Francis swung for the knock-out blow, I ducked, connected with my left, and finished him off with my right. Francis hit the floor like a rock. It happened so fast that Mother, with her failing eyesight, couldn't figure out what had happened. One minute Francis was standing there, the next he was gone!

That encounter gave Francis a healthy respect for me. He never bothered me again, and neither did my other brothers.

Just as I got the better of Francis, my sibling rival, so too did Merillat Woodworking Company surge ahead of its older and more experienced industry rivals. We began as underdogs, the newcomers on the block, a young company surrounded by others that had been in the business a long time. But we had the confidence of youth—we were lean, aggressive, innovative, and hungry for success. Other companies were resting on their laurels, their seniority, or their market share. But we didn't have that luxury.

By 1973 Merillat Woodworking ranked fifteenth among the nation's cabinet producers. The Adrian plant employed 300 people who produced 1,600 cabinets every day. But while being number fifteen was nice, it still wasn't nice enough. We wanted to be number one, and we were willing to try a lot of new things to get there. We even gave the company a new name to reflect our vision for growth and expansion, a name which could encompass far more than woodworking. We became Merillat Industries, Inc.

The Mother of Invention

Much of our success up to this point could be attributed to God-given ideas—like the self-closing hinge, the drawer guide, and the Trust and Share Program. Now, another major innovation—actually a revolutionary idea—spurred us on to much greater heights. For that, God's guiding hand took me to a most unlikely place: Singapore.

During those years I was scouring the world for plywood to keep the company going. When production grows, it takes more supplies to feed the system. A growing manufacturing business is a hungry beast which must constantly be fed, and the bigger it grows, the more it needs. These trips took me to such places as Finland, Tokyo, Taiwan, Hong Kong, and finally, Singapore.

On a trip to Singapore, I discovered a mill with a warehouse full of plywood. Yet they were complaining that they didn't have enough plywood to ship to America. I saw through this ruse. By claiming there was a shortage, they could charge higher prices.

Up until that moment, our business and our industry

had been hostage to Asian suppliers. I decided then and there that somehow I would break our dependency on foreign plywood. And during the long flight from Singapore to San Francisco, I started designing a line of cabinetry that consisted entirely of American-made materials.

What could I use instead of plywood? I asked myself. Most of America's timber was oak. It was very hard and had a beautiful wood grain, so I decided it would work fine for the doors and front trim. For the rest of the cabinet I would use particleboard. The supply was plentiful; it was made from wood shavings and scraps. To make the particleboard more attractive, I could cover it with vinyl.

By using oak, particleboard, and vinyl, I could cut those greedy overseas suppliers out of most of the production process. If my plan was right, it just might work.

And so it did. It worked so well, in fact, that the increased business prompted me to build another factory. But where to build this time? Studying the situation, I devised some guidelines that proved to be successful and would be suitable for any business or industry considering plant location and start-up.

1. Find a place with the desired natural resources available in the immediate area.

2. Select a site with good highway access and with plenty of land for expansion.

3. Have the Chamber of Commerce check wage rates of ten companies that employ the number of people you plan to employ within a thirty-mile radius of the proposed plant site. Drop the top two wage rates. Average the other eight and pay within that range with future incentives.

4. When employing your work force, advise them that you are using an "all-salaried" plan.

5. After the personnel manager has interviewed and offered workers employment, let it be known that you trust them. As a rule, only five percent of the workers hired will have been a mistake. Management's job is to turn the five percent into believers or leavers.

6. Give management a year to form a top-notch production team, then install the employee incentive plan, using that level of production as your base.

7. Establish a policy to pay suppliers within ten days. Nothing is better for promoting good business relationships.

8. Purchase up-to-date equipment with profits to increase production.

After extensive surveys, Ruth and I decided that Jackson, Ohio, looked like the best place. Merillat Industries purchased land and built a 105,000 square-foot plant to pre-dry one million board feet per month. We bought kilns to dry 35,000 board feet per day. The rest of the plant processed the wood into cabinet frames and parts. These elements were then assembled, finished, packaged, and shipped to Adrian.

Amazingly enough, we soon realized that we needed another plant to produce doors and fronts to allow the Jackson plant to focus solely on producing frames. The search process began again, and this time we settled on Atkins, Virginia, a town we had come across during an earlier search. In 1978 we began building a plant almost identical to the one in Jackson, though a bit larger—184,000 feet.

In both places, start-up had its usual problems. But

we were fortunate in being able to employ outstanding people who wanted to be part of the team. Implementation of the all-salaried plan eliminated half the normal start-up problems.

The increased demand for cabinets required more assembly plants and for that we built an addition to the Adrian plant and strategically purchased another plant in Lakeville, Minnesota.

The growth continued year after year.

In 1977 I was voted Michigan's Small Businessman of the Year. I went to Washington, D.C., to compete for the national title, but lost out to another notable businessman from Plains, Georgia.

Investing in Young People

During all of this growth, we continued practicing the principles of Malachi 3:10, giving one-tenth of everything we made to the Lord's work. Ruth and I saw the promise of that verse fulfilled and multiplied year by year as God did indeed pour out such a blessing we could not contain it. It was humbling to see how God was using us for His purposes, and it was amazing to see what we had been able to do with a little wood and a commitment to Him.

Our giving, of course, increased as the business grew. But we didn't just sit back and write out checks to the church, thinking nothing more should be expected of us. Despite the time demands of our growing business, we became more and more involved in the work of our church.

I was asked to teach a Sunday school class, a task to which I committed myself for thirty years. More than once, I marveled that the children in my classes taught me more than I seemed to be teaching them.

One Sunday, the pastor invited members of the congregation to come up to the choir loft to help make a joyful noise to the Lord. Ruth and I went, and we really enjoyed it. I told Ruth, "From now on, let's always be there. At least there will always be two people to sing."

Ruth took this challenge seriously and became a mainstay of the music program in our church for over 30 years. What made that time so meaningful to her was that the messages in the songs they sang drew her closer to God. One song in particular remains dear to her heart: "To Be Used of God." This was always her desire—not to become wealthy or influential, but to be a servant for Him.

As the congregation grew in number, we began to realize the need for a new building. Ruth and I helped make that possible. But while we continued serving the Lord at the new Trenton Hills church, we also looked for other ways to store our treasure in heaven.

Even though I had achieved business success, I realized that the lack of a proper education had hindered some of the things I wanted to do. It was certainly a factor in preventing me from receiving my Coast Guard commission. Knowing that, I refused to boast, as some people in my position have done, "Who needs college? Look how I have succeeded without it."

I knew that such success stories wouldn't be as common in the future because the kind of education I never had is sorely needed for running a business in these times. Ruth and I could see the truth of that firsthand in the college

Inspecting the Merillat Industries plant in Atkins, Virginia. The plant produces doors, drawer fronts, and frames. TOP: Worker operates a large sanding machine. BOTTOM: Inspecting the panels.

TOP: Orville watches as workers operate a chop line.
BOTTOM: Orville takes a close look as the finish is applied.

graduates we hired to help run the company. Without those well-trained, well-educated people, Merillat Industries would certainly have suffered.

We were convinced that higher education was the way of the future. For that reason, Ruth and I decided to invest in the future of Christian young people everywhere by investing in Christian education. And it was only natural that we look first to Huntington College, a private Christian liberal arts college sponsored by our denomination, the Church of the United Brethren in Christ.

In the late 1960s we sold Cardinal of Adrian, the company we formed to produce the self-closing hinge, and invested the money in a new physical education center for Huntington College. It was the beginning of our long and very rewarding relationship with that school.

Our Growing Family

Of course, the young person we cared most about was our son, Richard. Like most proud parents, Ruth and I felt there was nothing too good for our son. When he was in high school, Richard met and fell in love with a pretty classmate named Lynette Jacobs.

After graduating from high school, Richard entered Huntington College. But being his own man and wanting to get on with his life, he felt he was spinning his wheels in college. He decided he wanted to come home and work for me. He called me one day and said, "Dad, I'll learn more about the kind of things I'm good at in the shop than I could ever learn in the classroom. I'm ready to come home."

Richard's desire to follow in my footsteps by learning

the cabinet-making business really made me proud. However, I was determined that he should go to college. In that area, at least, I didn't want him following in my footsteps. So, I agreed to let him come home on the condition that he transfer to Adrian College and finish his degree.

It was a deal. So Richard came home, and before long he and Lynette were married. He went to work at Merillat, and in 1971 they made Ruth and me grandparents by giving birth to our first grandchild, a sweet baby girl they named Wendy.

Before long, we made another investment in Christian education, this time much closer to home.

Because of the tremendous sales of cabinets, Ruth and I invested some of our profits in the stock market. A new fast-food chain opened a franchise about a half-mile from our office. We liked this place with the square hamburgers and the Frosty drinks, and we often ate lunch there. Thinking it might be a good investment, we bought stock in Wendy's.

That was in 1976. By this time, Richard and Lynette were going ahead with building plans of their own, having provided Wendy with two beautiful sisters, Collette and Tricia.

When I paused to realize that in another year our oldest grandchild would be starting school, I started thinking about the options. The record of public education wasn't very good in the mid-seventies, and it hasn't improved much since then. I was concerned about the welfare of our granddaughters, but also about the welfare of all the other children in our area. The deterioration of morals and ethics in the public school system seemed to be epidemic, so I asked God if there was something He wanted me to do about it. Once more, His guiding hand led the way.

Thanks to the rapid rise in value of Wendy's stock, we turned a very nice profit on our modest investment. With it, we funded a new Christian school in Adrian which taught children from a biblical, Christ-centered worldview. Since the school would be operated as an arm of our church, we named it Trenton Hills Christian School, and it started to grow immediately.

Bigger Business

In 1982 we discovered we needed a new corporate headquarters to coordinate management and day-to-day direction of all the various segments of Merillat Industries. We laid our plans carefully, organizing the management team and key players, and we built what is now our national headquarters. Located in Adrian, it serves as the corporation's communications and nerve center.

Distribution and demand required still more assembly plants, so in 1983 we built two more—one in Las Vegas, Nevada, and one in Culpeper, Virginia.

Then, getting really brave, Ruth and I considered building a particleboard plant. For this facility we chose Rapid City, South Dakota, a convenient location with a good supply base and transport links. We built a massive 406,000 square-foot plant which turns Ponderosa pine shavings into premium particleboard. The boards are laminated with vinyl and fabricated into components.

This new supplier showed us the need for another plant to produce frames and doors. After locating a site at Mt.

Jackson, Virginia, we took the plunge in 1985 and started yet another plant to manufacture door panels, drawer fronts, and frames to be sent to our other plants for assembly.

With business still growing, the goal continued to be supplying the distributors with the best cabinet value available. Our sales were growing at a compound rate of 24 percent each year.

In 1985 Merillat Industries became the number one cabinet maker in America, and my dream was fulfilled. The business had continued to expand rapidly, and Ruth and I knew, without a doubt, that God had enabled it all.

But just as everything was moving at breakneck speed, I suffered a stroke and landed in the hospital with my left side paralyzed. Ruth held a constant vigil at my side, and

Merillat Industries corporate headquarters in Adrian, Michigan.

after much therapy, I regained some of what I had lost—but not everything. In His providence, it seemed God was telling me I needed to slow down. After all, I had already reached retirement age.

It was clear something had to change. I couldn't run the company in my condition, and the old drive just wasn't there anymore. Unsure of what to do with the business, I asked God what He thought I should do. His answer, though difficult to handle, was clear. I had to sell.

The Lord sent two buyers who were interested in purchasing Merillat Industries, and in late 1985 the company was sold to Masco Corporation, a giant in the building-products industry. Masco saw no reason to meddle with success, so they pretty much left the company alone. I remained as Chairman, and my son, Richard, remained as President of the company. Merillat Industries continued operating under the same principles and ideals.

The sale of the company allowed Ruth and me to establish a charitable venture which we called the Christian Family Foundation. It was funded, in turn, by the Merillat Foundation which we had established to manage our various philanthropies. We had always been generous with our money, and this seemed to be the best way to make sure that our resources would be used for the glory of God in perpetuity. Since we attributed our success to God, we rejoiced at giving back to God. And especially now, as our involvement in the company decreased, we focused more and more of our attention on giving to the Lord's work—and unless you have done it, I cannot explain how incredibly rewarding this has been.

Over the years, we developed a few guidelines and we stick closely to them. As much as possible, we support projects within a 300-mile radius of Adrian. We insist on quality; if we're underwriting a building for the Lord's use, we want it to be done right. And we emphasize projects that benefit young people.

The Trenton Hills Christian School was such a project. We could see the immediate benefit, and it was a joy to see the school grow and thrive. However, in three short years the school was bursting at the seams. Response to the private school concept was so outstanding that Trenton Hills outgrew its facility and even a major addition to the school didn't solve the problem. To continue expanding, the school would need a new facility in a new location.

Ruth and I often drove by a spot in Adrian on US 223 that we thought would be an ideal place for a new building. The land seemed to be waiting for something special. With

The Lenawee Christian School in Adrian offers a modern, first-class education to some 700 students from kindergarten through twelfth grade.

money from the Merillat Foundation, we purchased the land and set to work.

On April 26, 1987, we dedicated the Lenawee Christian School. Whereas the previous school had been part of our church, this school became inter-denominational in scope and was operated by an elected school board. By 1991 this modern, first-class school had almost 700 students from pre-kindergarten through high school, with waiting lists at nearly every grade level.

Proving God's Bounty

After completing Lenawee Christian School, we starting working on the second phase of our plan for that property: the Christian Family Centre. It was built attached to the school complex, but was kept separate organizationally.

The vision for the Christian Family Centre arose from the Sunday school class I taught. I enjoyed the enthusiastic young people, but I realized they needed a place free of drinking, smoking, and swearing where they could go to have fun. I decided that if God made it possible, someday I would build a wholesome place where families could spend time together enjoying recreation and special programs.

The Christian Family Centre made this vision a reality. The facility includes a gymnasium, swimming pool, bowling alley, racquetball courts, a complete fitness center, a full-service restaurant with banquet facilities, and a 700-seat auditorium which hosts, as the recent Focus on the Family magazine article described it, a wide variety of top-notch family programming.

Over 4,000 members pay a nominal yearly membership fee to use the complex. Today, one of my favorite activities is coming to my office at the Centre and watching the families come in to play, eat, and just be together having fun.

The fact is, we've never lacked worthy causes. Huntington College needed some new dormitories, a library, and other facilities. During the mid 1980s the beautiful RichLyn Library and a couple of dormitories were completed. In 1990 the college dedicated its new centerpiece, the Merillat Centre for the Arts. There have been other projects along the way as the college has developed its long-range master plan, and we have been thrilled to help.

Among the other projects that have brought us special enjoyment are the new obstetrics ward at the Narsapur Hospital in India, a large Christian hospital headed by a United Brethren missionary and Camp Michindoh, a splendid Christian conference center and camp in Hillsdale, Michigan.

The Christian Family Centre, a state-of-the-art education and entertainment complex in Adrian, Michigan.

We have helped with the Farm Development Project in Sierra Leone, West Africa, and many other worthy causes. Even while God's guiding hand has provided us with much prosperity, He has also given us the joy of giving a portion of it right back to His work. However hard we try, the Lord just cannot be outdone.

Since our decision to apply Malachi 3:10 to our lives, Ruth and I have found that the more we give, the more God blesses us. Our family has been blessed, our giving has returned enormous blessings to us, and the growth of our company has been unimpeachable proof of God's bounty.

In 1986 Merillat Industries employed 2,500, with

Dedication plaque for the Merillat Maternity Ward at Narsapur Hospital in India. At right, Rev. Jerry Datema, the Overseas Bishop for the Church of the United Brethren in Christ, with his wife, Eleanor.

thousands more involved in distribution and sales supporting its manufacturing network. In that year alone, the industry sent 45 million quality cabinets to market.

Merillat Industries continues to be the country's number one cabinet maker, with its eleven plants located all around the country. All American-made, self-closing hinges are produced under license agreements stemming from my original patent. And all Merillat cabinets consist of the basic materials—oak, particle board, and vinyl—which I designed to produce a completely American-made product.

Unless you have given part of your life to a business, you may not understand my pride in these achievements. But for me, such successes are the evidence not of my wisdom but of God's blessing.

There is one other blessing I want to mention before bringing this story to a close. One of the great privileges of my life was the honor of delivering the Commencement address to the 1986 graduating class at Huntington College, the institution which holds such a dear place in my heart.

I don't know whether it was the irony of my own educational struggles or the knowledge that in this modern competitive age only those with the proper intellectual tools will make it. Nevertheless, there I was, a high school drop-out, imparting words of wisdom to a fine group of young people who, diplomas in hand, were ready to go out and make their own way in the world.

I wanted to touch them somehow, to share my heart, but what did I have to say to these bright young people? Well, I had a life of hard-won experience, I had been places, and I had a pretty good track record in the business world. As I told my story that day, I decided to tell them of God's guiding hand in my life, and to encourage them to rely on His guidance in their own, just as I had.

I closed my remarks with some simple principles which they may not have learned in the classroom, but which I hoped they would take to heart that Saturday afternoon in May. This is what I told them.

- People are unreasonable, illogical, and self-centered. But let God love them through you, anyway.
- If you do your best, people will accuse you of ulterior motives. Do your best, anyway.
- If you are successful, you may win false friends and true enemies. Succeed, anyway.
- Honesty and frankness make you vulnerable. Be honest and frank, anyway.
- The good you do today will be forgotten tomorrow. Do good, anyway. It'll let you sleep at night.
- People with the biggest dreams can be shot down by those with the smallest minds. Think big, anyway.
- What you spend years building may be destroyed over-night. Build, anyway.
- Give the world the best you've got, and you may get kicked in the teeth. Give the world the best you've got, anyway.
- In short, dare to be different from a lot of people you'll run into.
- If you do something worthy of remembrance, it'll be remembered.

SIX

Still Clutching His Hand

A S THE business world views it, Ruth and I are both well past retirement age, but we haven't retired from the Lord's service. Nobody ever does. Although we look back with satisfaction on all that God has allowed us to do, we're not content to sit back and relax. We have not yet done enough for Jesus Christ, considering all that He has done for us, especially through His death on a cross to give us eternal life with Him in heaven.

So we're still busy, working and giving for the King- dom. And we never forget that God's guiding hand, which has directed and protected our lives for the past 76 years, is

TOP: The Merillat family gathers for Christmas, 1988.
BOTTOM: Richard and Lynette with their daughters, from left, Tricia, Collette, and Wendy (Scott Hall Photography).

TOP: Orville celebrating a birthday with his granddaughters.
BOTTOM: Orville and Ruth's golden wedding anniversary
(Scott Hall Photography).

still leading us along. Wherever His guiding hand takes us in whatever years we have left, Ruth and I are content to go.

Parental love burns in my heart for my son, Richard, and his beautiful wife, Lynette. Richard is now president of the company Ruth and I spent most of our lives building. It could not be in better hands. My love also extends to our three grandchildren: Wendy, Collette, and Tricia. I wish each of them happiness and prosperity, and a life companion as godly and well-suited to their needs as the one God gave me. True love exchanged with one's life partner is more precious than gold.

I never stop thanking God for Ruth. She is truly God's gift to me. During our fifty-one years of marriage, she has always supported my ambition to provide the best for our customers. Not that we haven't disagreed at times; with so many decisions to make, we often looked at the proverbial elephant from different angles. But Ruth was always patient and would wait to bring up the issue during calmer circumstances. Blessed indeed is the person who can avoid conflicts.

Several life goals have arisen out of my Christian commitment. I have tried to share with others my love for Jesus Christ by my example, my words, and my actions. I have tried to fulfill a partnership role in my commitment to Ruth. And I have tried, with God's help, to be the very best I can be, so that I should never again bring shame to another person. These goals have been the principal factors in making the various choices I have described in these pages.

What we are is God's gift to us. We have all been blessed with a talent or skill that God expects us to perfect and share with others. But what we become, and how we use what He has given us, is our gift to God.

Still Clutching His Hand

For many years I have turned to Ruth for her input and insights in so many important undertakings. Now is certainly no time to change. So, in drawing this volume to a close, I would like to give my wife the final word by reciting something she said recently to friends of ours.

She said, "God has given Orville and me wealth and influence, and yet, everything we own belongs to God. We stand firmly on that principle, and refuse to budge from it. The Bible says, 'For unto whosoever much is given, of him shall much be required.' Since we have been given much, we realize God expects much from us. But we take joy in bearing that responsibility, and we pray daily that God will show us how to use what He has given us to help win the world for Christ."

Ruth went on to say, "While the company we founded will no doubt continue and prosper for many years to come, we have tried to operate from God's perspective, using the blessings of a successful company to make a difference in people's lives—a difference that lasts forever.

"I think this is the reason," she said, "why I cherish this two-line poem I learned so long ago. I believe it sums up perfectly why Orville and I have lived our lives the way we have."

Just one life, 'twill soon be past;
Only what's done for Christ will last.

Orville meets President Ronald Reagan, 1983.

The Measure of God's Blessing

THROUGHOUT their lives, Orville and Ruth Merillat have touched the lives of thousands. Their example and generous spirit have served to bring God's blessing to many people from a variety of backgrounds. A few of these people were asked to add their personal comments to the Merillats' story. Their responses are presented here.

I AM honored to join you in recognizing two citizens whose love of God and contributions to society deserve our highest praise—Orville and Ruth Merillat.

Orville and Ruth are truly citizens worthy of high praise and respect, for their faith and perseverance have helped advance the values we share and the hopes we cherish. Love of God, family, country, and neighbor has always been

Orville and Ruth with Vice President Dan Quayle, 1992.

the source of our strength and goodness as a nation. Time and time again, the Merillats have stood tall in defense of these values.

Sacred Scripture teaches all of us to lead lives that will serve as an example to others. The vision, faith, and devotion that Orville and Ruth Merillat have shown through their lives serve as a source of strength for all people at a time when it is sorely needed. It will be an example for generations to come.

Marilyn and I join you in thanking Orville and Ruth for all they have done, and continue to do, to make this country the more decent land we want it to be. May the light of the Lord's love guide them always.

Dan Quayle
Vice President of the United States

*   *   *

THE PIONEERS, inventors, and industrialists that brought material wealth to this nation and the world arose from an environment that prized honesty, thrift, excellence, and innovation. In every generation there are outstanding men and women who embody these virtues and lead lives committed to them. Orville and Ruth Merillat are two such people.

Their success as individuals, as parents, and as entrepreneurs illustrates what made America a good and great nation. They are but two of the millions of individuals, who, by hard work and faith, not government largesse, achieved success during their lifetime and helped to make our republic to prosper.

They have not kept the fruits of their labors to

themselves. Schools, churches, missionary organizations, and a host of other worthy causes are the recipients of their generous gifts. I want to commend the Merillats, in particular, for their willingness to help shoulder the financial burden of private education. Their support helps ensure a thriving alternative to our badly failing public education system.

William Bennett
Former Secretary of Education
Washington, D.C.

*   *   *

LOAVES AND fishes really do multiply when we place them in the Lord's hands! Veterans will tell you that there are real adventures and surprises ahead for anyone bold enough to dig up the talent and bring the tithe into the storehouse. This institution offers geometrical interest rates!

Orville Merillat has staked his life on that axiom, and proven it over and over again. I know, because Focus on the Family has been the beneficiary of his faithfulness! At first glance, the Merillats simply appear to be extremely generous. But there's more to this story—a deeper motivation behind the giving, the support, the involvement, the astounding investment in other people's lives and ministries. It's this conviction that God is alive and that He supernaturally increases the effect of the gifts we lay in His lap until the windows of heaven burst open and the blessings pour down like rain!

James C. Dobson, Ph.D.
President, Focus on the Family
Colorado Springs, Colorado

The Measure of God's Blessing

*   *   *

I AM delighted to say a word of praise concerning the life and mission of Orville and Ruth Merillat. They have taken the same tender care of God's ministry as they initially brought to the business of making quality cabinets. These two people do not segment their lives. They are not Christians on Sunday and something else on Monday. Their entire lives—professionally, personally, spiritually, and intellectually—have been dedicated to the work of the Kingdom.

> Robert A. Seiple
> President, World Vision
> Monrovia, California

*   *   *

I REMEMBER well the first time we met and the gracious way in which you listened as I shared with you my burden for evangelical cooperation through the National Association for Evangelicals.

I rejoice in how God has used you to touch the lives of others and the humility with which you have shared the resources He has placed in your hands. Because of your faithfulness, God's Word will be planted in the hearts of generations to come to the glory and honor of Jesus Christ.

> Billy A. Melvin
> Executive Director
> National Association of Evangelicals
> Carol Stream, Illinois

*   *   *

AT THE Family Research Council, we are fighting every day for the American family because we believe that it is God's ordained institution for the care, nurturance, and propagation of His people. In the successes we have had in defending the family in the public arena, we pray that in some small way we are contributing to God's plan for America.

It is these successes that Orville Merillat can point to as part of his legacy to his own family and millions of other families across our nation. The liberal establishment has control of the power centers of our country: the intelligentsia, the business community, the media, and the political establishment. With his generous contributions to the ongoing work of the Family Research Council, Orville Merillat has been a fundamental part of fighting back. He has expanded our resources and enabled us to continue the essential task of promoting family values in our nation's capital.

As God has kept His guiding hand on Orville Merillat's life, Orville has in turn reached his hands out to others. Just as Psalm 62:10 admonished, "If riches increase, Do not set your heart on them," Orville has set his heart on using his resources to strengthen the family—to leave a heritage of lasting value. This is a measure of true wealth: a man who can survey his life and see investments of enduring significance. Orville Merillat is such a man, for surely the family is an investment of inestimable worth.

Gary L. Bauer
President, Family Research Council
Washington, D.C.

The Measure of God's Blessing

*   *   *

THE MINISTRIES of Youth for Christ around the world have been greatly enhanced through the faithful stewardship of Orville D. Merillat.

Orville Merillat is a Christian statesman of the highest caliber. His spirit of humility; aggressive, entrepreneurial leadership; and faithful stewardship of the blessings of God in his life are all making very significant contributions to the work of God's kingdom. He is a model to both the business world and Christian leaders.

My personal life and the ministries of Youth for Christ are greatly enriched through our associations with Orville D. Merillat.

> Dr. Richard R. Wynn
> Asia-Pacific Area Director
> Youth for Christ International
> Singapore

*   *   *

IDEA BY idea and project by project, Orville and Ruth Merillat have been our prime allies in developing a state-of-the-art twenty-first-century campus. Simply put, without their involvement, the new "Huntington College" would simply have been a figment of our collective imaginations. The Board's vision for the campus, coupled with the Merillat's faithfulness and God's multitude of blessings have resulted in eight major projects on the Huntington campus since the early 1980s. We have been the beneficiaries of Malachi 3:10 as we have shared in God's blessings to the Merillats.

Do we feel blessed for having had the privilege of being partners with these incredible people? Absolutely. Do we feel humbled by seeing God's hand on their lives? Most certainly. What never ceases to amaze me is God's blessing and use of faithful people whom He can trust. As a result, His blessings touch the lives of people for generations to come, worldwide.

> Eugene B. Habecker
> President, Huntington College (1981-1991)
> President, American Bible Society
> New York, New York

*   *   *

MICHIGAN FAMILY FORUM exists to encourage Michigan's government, churches, and families to perform their God-ordained role toward the promotion of responsible citizenship. Through the incredible generosity and encouragement of Orville and Ruth, we have been able to dream great dreams and pursue the significant vision that God has given us to call our state and nation back to allegiance to God and His principles for mankind. Anything short of this will merely be cosmetic, providing, at best, a momentary lull in the storm.

In addition to their financial assistance, the Merillats, despite ill-health and physical weakness, continue making a difference in this world with youthful enthusiasm. While many retired people seek earthly reward for their endeavors in this life, Orville and Ruth are content to follow the biblical example of laying up treasures in heaven where they will enjoy their reward for all eternity.

> Randall J. Hekman
> Executive Director
> Michigan Family Forum
> Lansing, Michigan

*   *   *

YOUR MANY friends at Boysville of Michigan would like to add their testimony about the many Michigan youth and families who have benefited and received blessings from the Lord through your active involvement in Boysville's programs.

Your encouragement and support of our family program has brought special blessings to many of our state families: people who needed help to understand their parental responsibilities and their need to recommit themselves to each other and to their children.

We are thankful for the Lord's blessing and for the opportunity to work together for His end.

> Brother Francis Boylan, csc
> Executive Director
> Boysville of Michigan
> Southfield, Michigan

*   *   *

YES, ORVILLE has been extremely successful and God has rewarded him wonderfully and Michidoh Ministries Camp and

Conference Center has reaped the benefits. Orville placed God first and God opened the floodgates of heaven with His blessings on His faithful servant Orville, who is now giving it all back to his Creator.

I know that the fruits of Orville's efforts will be seen by many for years to come in the brick and mortar of his accomplishments, but his testimony will remain forever in the hearts he has touched.

Orville has a title and yes, he will be remembered as the founder of a great and successful company, but his testimony to Jesus Christ will carry him unto our Father.

Cliff D. Miller, Chief Executive Officer
Michindoh Ministries Camp and Conference Center
Hillsdale, Michigan

*   *   *

THE ACHIEVEMENTS of this remarkable man's life bear living testimony to the truth of Malachi 3:10. Orville's personal relationship with Christ, his faithfulness to the Lord's teachings, have resulted in a cascade of blessings.

But perhaps the greatest blessing of our friendship comes from the inspiration of just knowing him. Christ made it clear that the best teacher is the living example, and that fits Orville to a "T." How does one know that if one lives his life as the Lord would have it, that the Lord will, in fact, "open the windows of heaven and pour out a blessing until it overflows?" My answer to that is, just look at Orville Merillat and the countless people who have been blessed because of his work: thousands of employees, millions of consumers, hundreds of families, and on and on it goes.

Orville Merillat is precisely what Malachi 3:10 is all about.

Lawrence W. Reed
President, The Mackinac Center
Midland, Michigan

*   *   *

IT TAKES a special kind of person to build an internationally-known company—a man who is decisive, innovative, driven, hard-working, visionary, and who has business savvy. I have seen all of those qualities in Orville Merillat, and I wish I shared those qualities to a greater extent.

But there is much more to Orville Merillat. There is the tender-hearted man whose voice easily cracks as he talks about Ruth, his family, or how God has worked in his life. The principled man, who knows what he believes and stands firm and unshakable on his convictions. The wise man, whose common-sense advice and perceptions have given me superb insights into the church and church leadershp—even though I'm the one who is supposed to be the expert in that field.

And there is the devoted husband, who treated his wife as a respected equal partner decades before the rest of society realized that's the way it should be. Whether it's receiving an honorary degree or being recognized as National Association of Evangelicals Layperson of the Year, Orville insists that Ruth stand at his side as a co-recipient. It's both, or none. Orville says he couldn't have done it without Ruth. And knowing Ruth, I have to agree.

C. Ray Miller, Bishop
Church of the United Brethren in Christ
Huntington, Indiana

*   *   *

AS A trusted and faithful servant, Orville Merillat served as a catalyst who helped make good things happen. The development of the Bixby Medical Center Renal Dialysis Center evolved because of his foresight and recognition of need. Today, it has served many patients locally who otherwise would have traveled great distances to gain access to this specialized care. In these ways, Orville Merillat has embodied the biblical injunction of a partner in Malachi 3:10.

His gift for goodness continues even further. When Bixby Medical Center outgrew its surgery facilities, Mr. Merillat served as a co-laborer and partner in the development of the new Merillat Surgery Center so that thousands of community residents could benefit from the result of improved access to sophisticated surgical services. His activism follows one of his guiding principles: to give something back to the community where he has lived and worked. In doing so, his work has allowed Bixby Medical Center to upgrade the quality of service, comfort, and care for all in need.

The Merillat Surgery Center stands not only as a legacy for one of God's faithful servants, but also as a beacon of light for the sick and infirmed.

The Measure of God's Blessing

Douglas W. McNeill, FACHE
President and C.E.O.
Bixby Medical Center
Adrian, Michigan

*   *   *

OVER THE years that I have been associated with Lenawee Christian School, God has abundantly poured out blessings upon my life. One of the blessings that has affected me most is getting to know Orville and Ruth Merillat. This couple possesses qualities that set them apart in our world today.

I am only one of thousands of people whose lives have been enriched by knowing Orville and Ruth Merillat. They have allowed God to use their lives to reflect His love and care, not only to this generation, but to the generations to come. Thank you to the Merillats for allowing God to work through them.

Paul R. Palpant
Elementary Administrator
Lenawee Christian School
Adrian, Michigan

*   *   *

I HAVE had the opportunity to meet with Mr. and Mr. Merillat on a number of occasions. I thank God for the model of their lives and for their friendship. Their commitment to one another in strong marriage, their commitment to their local church, to their denominations, and to the people whom God has brought into their lives means so much to me.

Doug Birdsall
President, LIFE Ministries
San Dimas, California

*   *   *

ONE WOULD have to look a long way in American life to find a comparable story. Ruth and Orville have left their mark on their trade by the creative use of their skills. They have made a significant impact on the world of education and culture by the liberality of their largesse. Their influence has touched thousands because of their spirit.

What accounts for all of this? Orville Merillat is a skilled and creative carpenter and Ruth is his equally capable teammate. The real key to their influence is the fact that for most of their life together they have taken their cues from another carpenter. The grace that was brought into the world in Jesus of Nazareth has broken into these two. And the Spirit that moved in this One whom they call "Lord" moves in them too. As He has given, they also have given. Many in our world are the richer for it. Those of us who are beneficiaries can only say, "Thank you, Lord, for Ruth and Orville."

Dennis F. Kinlaw
Chancellor
Asbury College
Wilmore, Kentucky

The Measure of God's Blessing

*   *   *

WE OF THE Christian College Coalition join with many friends in expressing our sincere gratitude for your vision and your stewardship.

Beyond the very significant Christian Family Centre in Adrian, Michigan, the numerous campus developments that you have funded, your partnership with the Christian College Coalition is touching eighty-three campuses and is blessing thousands of faculty and nearly 100,000 students. With you, we believe that preparing young people to serve Christ in life is one of the greater missions for His Kingdom. Through training young people to be informed disciples of Christ we will improve our nation and the world.

> Myron S. Augsburger
> President, Christian College Coalition
> Washington, D.C.

*   *   *

IN OUR modern times with its empty worldly distractions, we think all too infrequently about what T. S. Eliot termed "the permanent things" which call us to a higher order of living. Ruth and Orville have shown us that the strength of the family, the liberty granted by our Constitution, the work ethic encouraged by our free enterprise system, and the gift of our Christian faith provide the lasting elements of a life worth living. Together the Merillat's Lenawee Christian School and Christian Family Centre, along with our work at Hillsdale College, seek to instill in our students an understanding of citizenship and stewardship.

Through our students, an opportunity is provided, a door is opened, and a difference can be made. Ruth and Orville have labored tirelessly in this noble task.

> George Roche
> President, Hillsdale College
> Hillsdale, Michigan

*   *   *

I HAVE HAD the privilege of knowing the Merillats for nearly three years, my tenure as president of Adrian College. I admire greatly their commitment to making a positive difference in the lives of others. They also understand the importance of helping young people to develop balanced lives, to gain the intellectual, physical, moral, and spiritual strength necessary to live productive lives of service to others and to God.

I am also impressed with the Christian humility they exhibit. Orville and Ruth Merillat have done so much for so many that they might be justified in boasting of their accomplishments and seeking the praise they merit. This is certainly the custom of the day. Instead they show us the meaning of true humility as they express gratitude for their good fortune and garner quiet satisfaction from the good things which their philanthropy has accomplished.

> Stanley P. Caine
> President, Adrian College
> Adrian, Michigan

*   *   *

BEGINNING FROM the rich soil of this rural Michigan county,

The Measure of God's Blessing

Ruth and Orville have worked for many years to demonstrate by the conduct of their lives the Scriptural admonitions to pray, live for, and seek the Lord in all things.

No better example of this is the emphasis that Mr. and Mrs. Merillat have placed on private Christian education. Both in their own Lenawee Christian School and the many other church-related elementary, secondary, and higher education institutions they have supported, Orville and Ruth have expressed a common theme: that the means which God has entrusted to them in this life be used in the most prudent way to guide people to their next life with our Creator.

Sister Cathleen Real, C.H.M.
President, Siena Heights College
Adrian, Michigan

*   *   *

I HAVE known Orville and Ruth Merillat for only a brief time, but on numerous occasions with them I have been impressed by their love for the Lord. Their commitment to their Lord and Savior, Jesus Christ, and their desire to do His will have led them to their financial investments in the work of the kingdom. They have been true servants, giving as the Lord has directed them. They have taken to heart and practiced Paul's words, "Now it is required that those who have been given a trust must prove faithful" (1 Corinthians 4:2 NIV). Their giving has been a practical expression of their deep Christian faith.

G. Blair Dowden
President, Huntington College
Huntington, Indiana

*   *   *

I HAVE been blessed by God to know and observe Orville and Ruth Merillat. Their influence and actions have produced several blessings in my life.

One blessing is to have been an observer of a true visionary. There must be the idea, the germ of a vision, that awaits a man to "see" the future. Then the motivation can begin for a concerted effort to accomplish the future. This blessing has propelled me to discover the future as God would have it, and then seek the people who would participate and work the dream into reality.

Another blessing received from this remarkable man is his ability to invest in the long term. Eternal is a better word for it! I have been blessed to see an example of giving up the things of this life, for what cannot be bought. Devotion to the souls of people, and to the furthering of people, can be seen in every building project that I have come in contact with. Body, mind, and soul are reflected in the architecture, purpose, and activity of the disbursed funding of a very successful career. I have been blessed to see a man who placed his Lord above an ability to be a lord.

Pastor Daniel A. Maas
Trenton Hill United Brethren Church
Adrian, Michigan